Osnabrücker Bibliografie:
Genremalerei des 19. Jahrhunderts
USA und Europa
19th century genre painting
USA and Europe

Stefanie Lipke

Osnabrücker Bibliografie:

Genremalerei des 19. Jahrhunderts
USA und Europa
19th century genre painting
USA and Europe

Verlag Dirk Koentopp

Lipke, Stefanie
Osnabrücker Bibliografie:
Genremalerei des 19. Jahrhunderts - USA und Europa
19th century genre painting - USA and Europe
Osnabrück: Verlag Dirk Koentopp, 2012
ISBN 978-3-938342-30-5

ISBN 978-3-938342-30-5

© 2012 Verlag Dirk Koentopp, Osnabrück
Das Werk einschließlich aller seiner Teile ist urheberrechtlich geschützt. Jede Verwertung außerhalb der engen Grenzen des Urheberrechtsgesetzes ist ohne Zustimmung des Verlages unzulässig und strafbar. Das gilt insbesondere für Vervielfältigungen, Übersetzungen, Mikroverfilmungen und die Einspeicherung und Verarbeitung in elektronischen Systemen.
Herstellung: Books on Demand GmbH

Printed in Germany

Inhaltsverzeichnis

Einleitung	**1**
1. Genremalerei als Bildgattung	**5**
2. Genremalerei im Vergleich (Europa und USA)	**7**
2.1 Europa und USA	7
2.2 Europa	7
2.3 Frankreich und Großbritannien	8
2.4 Frankreich und USA	8
2.5 Deutschland und USA	9
2.6 Deutschland und England	9
2.7 Spezielle Themenbereiche	9
3. Genremalerei in Europa	**11**
3.1 Deutschland	11
3.1.1 Malerei des 19. Jahrhunderts	11
3.1.2 Genremalerei	11
3.1.2.1 Überblick	11
3.1.2.2 Die Düsseldorfer Malerschule	13
3.1.2.3 Regionale Malerei	13
3.1.2.3.1 Norddeutschland	13
3.1.2.3.2 Rhein-Main Gebiet	14
3.1.2.3.3 Süddeutschland	14
3.1.2.4 Spezielle Themenbereiche	15
3.1.3 Künstler	16
3.1.3.1 Ferdinand Brütt	16
3.1.3.2 Heinrich Bürkel	17
3.1.3.3 Franz Ludwig Catel	17
3.1.3.4 Johann Peter Hasenclever	17
3.1.3.5 Carl Wilhelm Hübner	17
3.1.3.6 Ludwig Knaus	18

3.1.3.7 Max Liebermann 18
3.1.3.8 Adolph Menzel 19
3.1.3.9 Moritz Daniel Oppenheim 19
3.1.3.10 Hubert Salentin 19
3.1.3.11 Theodor Schütz 20
3.1.3.12 Reinhard Sebastian Zimmermann 20
3.1.3.13 Sonstige 20

3.2 Frankreich 24
  3.2.1 Malerei des 19. Jahrhunderts 24
  3.2.2 Genremalerei 24
  3.2.3 Künstler 25
    3.2.3.1 Louis-Leopold Boilly 25
    3.2.3.2 Jules Breton 26
    3.2.3.3 Ernest Meissonier 26
    3.2.3.4 Jean-Francois Millet 26
    3.2.3.5 Sonstige 27

3.3 Griechenland 28

3.4 Großbritannien 29
  3.4.1 England 29
    3.4.1.1 Malerei des 19. Jahrhunderts 29
    3.4.1.2 Genremalerei 29
      3.4.1.2.1 Überblick 29
      3.4.1.2.2 Spezielle Themenbereiche 30
    3.4.1.3 Künstler 31
      3.4.1.3.1 William Powell Frith 31
      3.4.1.3.2 Sonstige 32
  3.4.2 Schottland 33
    3.4.2.1 Überblick 33
    3.4.2.2 Künstler 33
      3.4.2.2.1 David Wilkie 33

3.5 Irland 34
  3.5.1 Überblick 34
  3.5.2 Künstler 34

3.6 Italien	35
3.6.1 Überblick	35
3.6.2 Regionale Malerei	35
3.6.2.1 Abruzzen	35
3.6.2.2 Kampanien	36
3.6.2.3 Toskana	36
3.6.2.4 Venetien und Lombardei	36
3.6.3 Künstler	36
3.6.3.1 Domenico Induno	36
3.6.3.2 Sonstige	37
3.7 Niederlande	38
3.8 Polen	39
3.9 Russland	40
3.9.1 Überblick	40
3.9.2 Künstler	41
3.10 Schweiz	42
3.10.1 Überblick	42
3.10.2 Künstler	42
3.10.2.1 Albert Anker	42
3.10.2.2 Raphael Ritz	42
3.10.2.3 Sonstige	43
3.11 Skandinavien	44
3.11.1 Überblick	44
3.11.2 Dänemark	44
3.11.3 Norwegen	44
3.11.4 Schweden	45
3.12 Spanien	46
3.12.1 Überblick	46
3.12.2 Regionale Genremalerei	46
3.12.2.1 Andalusien	46
3.12.2.2 Kanarische Inseln	46

3.12.3 Künstler 47

3.13 Ungarn 48

3.14 Österreich 49
   3.14.1 Überblick 49
   3.14.2 Künstler 49
      3.14.2.1 Josef Danhauser 49
      3.14.2.2 Franz von Defregger 50
      3.14.2.3 Eduard von Engerth 50
      3.14.2.4 Peter Fendi 50
      3.14.2.5 Mathias Schmid 51
      3.14.2.6 Ferdinand Georg Waldmüller 51
      3.14.2.7 Sonstige 52

3.15 Weitere europäische Länder 53

4. Genremalerei in den USA **55**
4.1 Malerei des 19. Jahrhunderts 55
4.2 Genremalerei 56
   4.2.1 Überblick 56
   4.2.2 Regionale Genremalerei 58
   4.2.3 Spezielle Themenbereiche 59
4.3 Künstler 60
   4.3.1 George Caleb Bingham 60
   4.3.2 John George Brown 61
   4.3.3 Francis William Edmonds 61
   4.3.4 Seymour Joseph Guy 62
   4.3.5 Winslow Homer 62
   4.3.6 Thomas Hovenden 63
   4.3.7 Henry Inman 63
   4.3.8 Eastman Johnson 63
   4.3.9 John Lewis Krimmel 64
   4.3.10 William Sidney Mount 64
   4.3.11 William Ranney 66
   4.3.12 Lilly Martin Spencer 66

4.3.13 Jerome Thompson	67
4.3.14 Richard Caton Woodville	67
4.3.15 Sonstige	67
5. Asien und Südamerika	**69**
5.1 Asien	69
5.2 Südamerika	70
5.2.1 Mexiko	70

Contents

Introduction	3
1. Genre painting as a category of painting	5
2. Genre painting in comparison (Europe and USA)	7
2.1 Europe and USA	7
2.2 Europe	7
2.3 France and Great Britain	8
2.4 France and USA	8
2.5 Germany and USA	9
2.6 Germany and England	9
2.7 Specific subject areas	9
3. Genre painting in Europe	11
3.1 Germany	11
3.1.1 19th century painting	11
3.1.2 Genre painting	11
3.1.2.1 General works	11
3.1.2.2 Düsseldorf school of painting	13
3.1.2.3 Regional painting	13
3.1.2.3.1 Northern Germany	13
3.1.2.3.2 Rhine-Main area	14
3.1.2.3.3 Southern Germany	14
3.1.2.4 Specific subject areas	15
3.1.3 Artists	16
3.1.3.1 Ferdinand Brütt	16
3.1.3.2 Heinrich Bürkel	17
3.1.3.3 Franz Ludwig Catel	17
3.1.3.4 Johann Peter Hasenclever	17
3.1.3.5 Carl Wilhelm Hübner	17
3.1.3.6 Ludwig Knaus	18

3.1.3.7 Max Liebermann	18
3.1.3.8 Adolph Menzel	19
3.1.3.9 Moritz Daniel Oppenheim	19
3.1.3.10 Hubert Salentin	19
3.1.3.11 Theodor Schütz	20
3.1.3.12 Reinhard Sebastian Zimmermann	20
3.1.3.13 Others	20
3.2 France	24
3.2.1 19th century painting	24
3.2.2 Genre painting	24
3.2.3 Artists	25
3.2.3.1 Louis-Leopold Boilly	25
3.2.3.2 Jules Breton	26
3.2.3.3 Ernest Meissonier	26
3.2.3.4 Jean-Francois Millet	26
3.2.3.5 Others	27
3.3 Greece	28
3.4 Great Britain	29
3.4.1 England	29
3.4.1.1 19th century painting	29
3.4.1.2 Genre painting	29
3.4.1.2.1 General works	29
3.4.1.2.2 Specific subject area	30
3.4.1.3 Artists	31
3.4.1.3.1 William Powell Frith	31
3.4.1.3.2 Others	32
3.4.2 Scotland	33
3.4.2.1 General works	33
3.4.2.2 Artists	33
3.4.2.2.1 David Wilkie	33
3.5 Ireland	34
3.5.1 General works	34
3.5.2 Artists	34

3.6 Italy	35
3.6.1 General works	35
3.6.2 Regional painting	35
3.6.2.1 Abruzzo	35
3.6.2.2 Campania	36
3.6.2.3 Tuscany	36
3.6.2.4 Veneto and Lombardy	36
3.6.3 Artists	36
3.6.3.1 Domenico Induno	36
3.6.3.2 Others	37
3.7 Netherlands	38
3.8 Poland	39
3.9 Russia	40
3.9.1 General works	40
3.9.2 Artists	41
3.10 Switzerland	42
3.10.1 General works	42
3.10.2 Artists	42
3.10.2.1 Albert Anker	42
3.10.2.2 Raphael Ritz	42
3.10.2.3 Others	43
3.11 Scandinavia	44
3.11.1. General works	44
3.11.2 Denmark	44
3.11.3 Norway	44
3.11.4 Sweden	45
3.12 Spain	46
3.12.1 General works	46
3.12.2 Regional genre painting	46
3.12.2.1 Andalusia	46
3.12.2.2 Canary Islands	46

3.12.3 Artists	47
3.13 Hungary	48
3.14 Austria	49
3.14.1 General works	49
3.14.2 Artists	49
3.14.2.1 Josef Danhauser	49
3.14.2.2 Franz von Defregger	50
3.14.2.3 Eduard von Engerth	50
3.14.2.4 Peter Fendi	50
3.14.2.5 Mathias Schmid	51
3.14.2.6 Ferdinand Georg Waldmüller	51
3.14.2.7 Others	52
3.15 Other European countries	53
4. Genre painting in the USA	**55**
4.1 19th century painting	55
4.2 Genre painting	56
4.2.1 General works	56
4.2.2 Regional genre painting	58
4.2.3 Specific subject areas	59
4.3 Artists	60
4.3.1 George Caleb Bingham	60
4.3.2 John George Brown	61
4.3.3 Francis William Edmonds	61
4.3.4 Seymour Joseph Guy	62
4.3.5 Winslow Homer	62
4.3.6 Thomas Hovenden	63
4.3.7 Henry Inman	63
4.3.8 Eastman Johnson	63
4.3.9 John Lewis Krimmel	64
4.3.10 William Sidney Mount	64
4.3.11 William Ranney	66
4.3.12 Lilly Martin Spencer	66

4.3.13 Jerome Thompson	67
4.3.14 Richard Caton Woodville	67
4.3.15 Others	67

5. Asia and South America   69
  5.1 Asia   69
  5.2 South America   70
    5.2.1 Mexico   70

Einleitung

Die vorliegende Bibliografie „Genremalerei des 19. Jahrhunderts – USA und Europa / 19th century genre painting – USA and Europe" mit ihren mehr als 500 Quellenangaben ist das Ergebnis einer umfangreichen Recherche in wissenschaftlichen Datenbanken und Bibliothekskatalogen weltweit. Sie soll einen Einstieg bieten in die Thematik der Genremalerei des 19. Jahrhunderts und ist zweisprachig, in Deutsch und Englisch, verfasst.

Neben Monografien und Sammelbänden wurden auch Aufsätze, sowohl aus Fachzeitschriften, als auch aus Sammelbänden in die Bibliografie mit aufgenommen.

Entsprechend der zweisprachigen Ausrichtung handelt es sich auch bei dem Großteil der im Folgenden aufgelisteten Titel um deutsch- und englischsprachige Literatur. Es wurden jedoch gemäß den in diesem Werk berücksichtigten europäischen Ländern, wie etwa Frankreich, Italien oder Spanien, zum Teil auch anderssprachige Werke mit einbezogen.

Die Bibliografie gliedert sich in insgesamt fünf Kapitel. Der erste Abschnitt beschäftigt sich als Einstieg allgemein mit dem Thema der Genremalerei als einer Gattung innerhalb der Malerei. Darauffolgend wurden Titel zusammengefasst, die einen ländervergleichenden Ansatz verfolgen. In Kapitel drei und vier werden dann die Länder Europas, sowie die USA einzeln aufgeführt, wobei es vor allem in diesen Bereichen weitere Untergliederungen gibt. So beginnen viele Abschnitte mit allgemeinen Titeln zu der Malerei des 19. Jahrhunderts und bieten somit einen guten Einstieg. Zudem wurden neben Überblickswerken und Werken zu spezifischen Themen der Genremalerei der entsprechenden Länder auch gesondert Titel zu einzelnen wichtigen Genremalern der Zeit aufgeführt, sodass ein schnelles Auffinden der passenden Literatur gewährleistet ist. Den Schluss der Bibliografie bildet dann ein kurzer Exkurs zu der Genremalerei in Asien und Südamerika.

Selbstverständlich kann auch in dieser Bibliografie kein Anspruch auf Vollständigkeit erhoben werden. Stattdessen soll dieses Werk zur weiteren Recherche und Beschäftigung mit der Thematik der Genremalerei animieren.

Introduction

The present bibliography „Genremalerei des 19. Jahrhunderts – USA und Europa / 19th century genre painting – USA and Europe" contains more than 500 bibliographical references and is the result of an extensive research in academic databases and library catalogues throughout the world. It is intended to serve as an introduction to the subject of 19th century genre painting and is written in both German and English.

Compiled in this volume are monographs and anthologies, as well as journal articles and essays from anthologies.

In accordance with the bilingual orientation the majority of the included works are German and English. However, due to the inclusion of European countries, like France, Italy or Spain, this bibliography also contains references of works written in other European languages.

The bibliography is organized into five basic sections. The first section focuses as an introduction on the subject of genre scenes as a category of painting. The following chapter contains works which are dedicated to a comparison of genre painting in different countries. The bibliographical references mentioned in section three and four are dealing with the individual European countries and the USA. Further subdivisions can be found in these two chapters which enable the reader to easily find the appropriate bibliographical references. This means that many sections begin as an introduction with general works concerning 19th century painting. In addition, a lot of subsections in part three and four focus on specific subject areas in genre painting as well as on individual genre painters. The concluding section of this volume is a short digression concerning genre painting in Asia and South America.

Of course, this bibliography does not claim completeness but is meant to initiate further interest in and research on the subject of genre painting.

1. Genremalerei als Bildgattung / Genre painting as a category of painting

Calvo Serraller, Francisco (2005): *Los géneros de la pintura*. Madrid: Taurus.

Elsig, Frédéric/ Darbellay, Laurent/ Kiss, Imola (Hrsg.) (2010): *Les genres picturaux: genèse, métamorphoses et transpositions*. Genève: Mé tispresses.

Gaehtgens, Barbara (Hrsg.) (2002): *Genremalerei. (Geschichte der klassischen Bildgattungen in Quellentexten und Kommentaren, Bd. 4)*. Berlin: Reimer.

Schneider, Norbert (2004): *Geschichte der Genremalerei. Die Entdeckung des Alltags in der Kunst der Frühen Neuzeit*. Berlin: Reimer.

Stechow, Wolfgang/ Comer, Christopher (1975/76): The History of the Term *Genre*; in: *Allen Memorial Art Museum Bulletin*, Bd. 33, Nr. 2, S. 89- 94.

2. Genremalerei im Vergleich (Europa und USA) / Genre painting in comparison (Europe and USA)

2.1 Europa und USA / Europe and USA

Facos, Michelle (2011): *An introduction to nineteenth century art*. New York: Routledge.

Fontanel, Béatrice (2006): *Daily life in art*. New York: H.N. Abrams.

Guarisco Gallery (Hrsg.) (2001): *19th century genre*. Washington, DC: Guarisco Gallery.

Roters, Eberhard (1998): *Malerei des 19. Jahrhunderts: Themen und Motive*. (2 Bände) Köln: DuMont.

2.2 Europa / Europe

Bendigo Art Gallery (Hrsg.) (2002): *A primrose from England: 19th century narratives from the collection of the Bendigo Art Gallery*. (Ausst.-Kat.) Bendigo, Vic.: Bendigo Art Gallery.

Boyd, Rachel (Hrsg.) (2005): *Nineteenth century paintings*. London: Richard Green at Three London Galleries.

Cleveland Museum of Art (Hrsg.) (1999). *European paintings of the 19th century*. (two-volume set) Cleveland: Cleveland Museum of Art.

Hook, Philip/ Poltimore, Mark (1987): *Popular 19th century painting. A dictionary of European genre painters*. Woodbridge: Antique Collectors' Club.

Langdon, Helen (1979): *Everyday-life painting*. Oxford: Phaidon.

Lindemann, Bernd Wolfgang/ Santucci, Claudia (Hrsg.) (2002): *Vorbild Holland. Genre und Landschaft im 19. Jahrhundert: aus den Beständen des Kunstmuseums*. (Ausst.-Kat.) Basel: Kunstmuseum.

Llorens Serra, Tomás (Hrsg.) (1999): *Painting nature. Genre and landscape painting from Brueghel to Van Gogh: Carmen Thyssen-Bornemisza Collection. 1 October 1999 to 16 January 2000*. (Ausst.-Kat.) Madrid: Fundación Colección Thyssen-Bornemisza.

O'Mahony, Claire I.R. (2000): *Nineteenth century paintings.* (Ausst.-Kat.) London: Richard Green.

Schweers, Hans F. (1986): *Genrebilder in deutschen Museen. Verzeichnis der Künstler und Werke; mit 932 Abb.* München [u.a.]: Saur.

Washburn, Gordon Bailey (1954): *Pictures of everyday life. Genre painting in Europe, 1500- 1900.* (Ausst.-Kat.) Pittsburgh.

White, Keith Eric (1998): *Painters and Northern Europe's fisherfolk: late nineteenth century viewing expectations and artists representations of an ancient calling.* Diss. Univ. of London.

2.3 Frankreich und Großbritannien / France and Great Britain

George, Hardy (Hrsg.) (2005): *Artist as narrator. Nineteenth century narrative art in England and France.* (Ausst.-Kat.) Oklahoma City: Oklahoma City Museum of Art [u.a.].

Kepetzis, Ekaterini (2009): *Vergegenwärtigte Antike. Studien zur Gattungsüberschreitung in der französischen und englischen Malerei (1840- 1914).* Frankfurt am Main [u.a.]: Lang.

Morris, Edward (2005): *French art in nineteenth-century Britain.* New Haven, Conn./ London: Published for The Paul Mellon Centre for Studies in British Art by Yale University Press.

2.4 Frankreich und USA / France and USA

George, Hardy (2003): *Americans in Paris, 1850- 1910: the academy, the salon, the studio, and the artists' colony.* Oklahoma City, Okla.: Oklahoma City Museum of Art/ Seattle, Wash.: Distributed by the University of Washington Press.

Sturges, Hollister (Hrsg.) (1987): *The Rural vision. France and America in the late nineteenth century.* Omaha, Nebr.: Joslyn Art Museum.

Weisberg, Gabriel P. (1995): *Redefining genre. French and American painting 1850- 1900.* (Ausst.-Kat.) Seattle, Washington: University of Washington Press.

2.5 Deutschland und USA / Germany and USA

Bott, Katharina/ Bott, Gerhard (Hrsg.) (1996): *Vice versa. Deutsche Maler in Amerika – amerikanische Maler in Deutschland, 1813- 1913.* (Ausst.-Kat.) München: Hirmer.

Morgen, Sabine (2008): *Die Ausstrahlung der Düsseldorfer Schule nach Amerika im 19. Jahrhundert. Düsseldorfer Bilder in Amerika und amerikanische Maler in Düsseldorf. (Göttinger Beiträge zur Kunstgeschichte, Bd. 2).* Göttingen: Ed. Ruprecht.

2.6 Deutschland und England / Germany and England

Risch, Marianne (1986): *Die Druckgraphik englischer Genremaler und die Düsseldorfer Malerschule 1820- 1850.* Diss. Univ. Kiel.

2.7 Spezielle Themenbereiche / Specific subject areas

Brettell, Richard R./ Brettell, Caroline B. (1984): *Bäuerliches Leben. Seine Darstellung in der Malerei des 19. Jahrhunderts.* Genf: Skira. (Aus dem Englischen von Eva Gärtner)

Lucie-Smith, Edward/ Dars, Celestine A. (1976): *How the rich lived. The painter as witness, 1870- 1914.* New York [u.a.]: Paddington Press.

Lucie-Smith, Edward (1977): *Work and struggle: the painter as witness 1870- 1914.* New York: Paddington Press, distributed by Grosset & Dunlap.

Mayr-Oehring, Erika (Hrsg.) (2003): *Tischgesellschaften. Malerei des 16.- 20. Jahrhunderts.* Salzburg: Residenzgalerie.

Schürmann, Ulrich (1992): *Die Darstellung des alten Menschen in der Genremalerei des 19. Jahrhunderts.* Diss. Univ. Bonn.

Stukenbrock, Christiane (1993): *Frans Hals. Fröhliche Kinder, Musikanten und Zecher. Eine Studie zu ausgewählten Motivgruppen und deren Rezeptionsgeschichte. (Europäische Hochschulschriften: Reihe 28, Kunstgeschichte, Bd. 167).* Frankfurt am Main. [u.a.]: Lang.

3. Genremalerei in Europa / Genre painting in Europe

3.1 Deutschland / Germany

3.1.1 Malerei des 19. Jahrhunderts / 19th century painting

Buberl, Brigitte (Hrsg.) (2005): *Die Kleine Nationalgalerie. Ein Bildersaal deutscher Kunst im 19. Jahrhundert.* Köln: DuMont.

Gurock, Elisabeth (1990): *Fließende Gattungsgrenzen in der deutschen Kunstkritik und Malerei des 19. Jahrhunderts.* Diss. Univ. Münster (Westfalen).

Kohle, Hubertus (Hrsg.) (2008): *Geschichte der bildenden Kunst in Deutschland. Vom Biedermeier zum Impressionismus (Geschichte der bildenden Kunst in Deutschland. Bd. 7).* München [u.a.]: Prestel.

Locher, Hubert (2005): *Deutsche Malerei im 19. Jahrhundert.* Darmstadt: Wiss. Buchgesellschaft.

National Gallery, Great Britain/ Nationalgalerie, Germany (Hrsg.) (2001): *Spirit of an age: 19th century paintings from the Nationalgalerie, Berlin.* London: National Gallery.

Neidhardt, Hans Joachim (2008): *Deutsche Malerei des 19. Jahrhunderts.* Leipzig: Seemann.

Pfeiffer, Knut E. (1977): *Kunsttheorie und Kunstkritik im neunzehnten Jahrhundert. Das Beispiel Adalbert Stifter. (Bochumer Studien zur Publizistik- und Kommunikationswissenschaft, 11).* Bochum: Brockmeyer.

3.1.2 Genremalerei / Genre painting

3.1.2.1 Überblick / General works

Bisanz, Rudolf M. (Hrsg.) (1980): *The René von Schleinitz Collection of the Milwaukee Art Centre: major schools of German nineteenth-century painting.* Milwaukee: Milwaukee Art Center/ London: University of Wisconsin Press.

Czymmek, Götz (Hrsg.) (1983): *Aus Alltag und Geschichte. Genre- und Historienmalerei des 19. Jahrhunderts aus dem Besitz des Wallraf-Richartz-Museums.* (Ausst.-Kat.) Köln.

Edler, Doris (1992): *Vergessene Bilder. Die deutsche Genremalerei in den letzten Jahrzehnten des 19. Jahrhunderts und ihre Rezeption durch Kunstkritik und Publikum. (Kunstgeschichte, Bd. 13).* Münster [u.a.]: Lit.

Immel, Ute (1967): *Die deutsche Genremalerei im neunzehnten Jahrhundert.* Diss. phil. Univ. Heidelberg.

Landes, Lilian (2011): Volkslyrik, Kunstkritik, Feuilletonroman und Genremalerei. Über Annäherung und Austausch von Erfolgsformaten zwischen Literatur- und Kunstschaffenden des Vormärz, in: *Literaturbetrieb und Verlagswesen im Vormärz,* hrsg. von Christian Liedtke, Bielefeld: Aisthesis-Verl., S. 81- 101.

Norman, Geraldine (1987): *Die Maler des Biedermeier 1815- 1848. Beobachtete Wirklichkeit in Genre-, Porträt- und Landschaftsmalerei.* Freiburg im Breisgau [u.a.]: Herder. (Übertragung aus dem Englischen von Dagmar Naredi-Rainer)

Sitt, Martina/ Ricke-Immel, Ute (Hrsg.) (1996): *Angesichts des Alltäglichen. Genremotive in der Malerei zwischen 1830 und 1900. Aus dem Bestand des Kunstmuseums Düsseldorf im Ehrenhof mit Sammlung der Kunstakademie NRW.* (Ausst.-Kat.) Köln [u.a.]: Böhlau.

Steinle, Christa/ Danzer, Gudrun/ Peer, Peter (Hrsg.) (2006): *Zur Natur des Menschen. Genremalerei des 19. und frühen 20. Jahrhunderts. Aus der Sammlung der Neuen Galerie.* (Ausst.-Kat.) Weitra.

Teske, Reinhard (1976): *Studien zur Genremalerei im Vormärz.* Diss. Fachbereich Geschichts-, Sozial- u. Wirtschaftswiss. Univ. Stuttgart.

Ude, Karl (Hrsg.) (1975): *Maleridyllen. Die heile Welt des 19. Jahrhunderts.* München: Bruckmann.

Ude, Karl (1978): *Alltagsidylle in der Malerei des 19. Jahrhunderts.* München: Bruckmann.

3.1.2.2 Die Düsseldorfer Malerschule / Düsseldorf school of painting

Baumgärtel, Bettina (Hrsg.) (2011): *Die Düsseldorfer Malerschule und ihre internationale Ausstrahlung, 1819- 1918.* (Ausst.-Kat.) Petersberg: Imhof.

Cipa, Peter (1977): *Die Genremalerei der Düsseldorfer Malerschule zwischen 1830 und 1848. Unter besonderer Berücksichtigung des Werkes von Johann Peter Hasenclever.* Staatsarb. Univ. Bonn.

Fehlemann, Sabine (Hrsg.) (2003): *Das irdische Paradies – Sammlung Volmer.* (Ausst.-Kat.) Wuppertal: Von-der-Heydt-Museum.

Grewe, Cordula (1998): Sentiment und Sentimentalität in der Düsseldorfer Malerschule, in: *Weltkunst. Zeitschrift für Kunst und Antiquitäten,* Bd. 68, S. 2298- 2300.

Hütt, Wolfgang (1984): *Die Düsseldorfer Malerschule 1819- 1869.* Leipzig: Seemann.

Mai, Ekkehard (Hrsg.) (2010): *Mensch und Meer: Düsseldorfer Malerschule.* (Ausst.-Kat.) Bonn: Dr. Axe-Stiftung.

Mai, Ekkehard (2012): *Lebensbilder. Genremalerei der Düsseldorfer Malerschule.* Petersberg: Imhof.

Morgen, Sabine (2008): *Die Ausstrahlung der Düsseldorfer Schule nach Amerika im 19. Jahrhundert. Düsseldorfer Bilder in Amerika und amerikanische Maler in Düsseldorf. (Göttinger Beiträge zur Kunstgeschichte, Bd. 2).* Göttingen: Ed. Ruprecht.

Ricke-Immel, Ute (1979): Die Düsseldorfer Genremalerei, in: *Die Düsseldorfer Malerschule,* hrsg. von Wend von Kalnein, Mainz: Zabern, S. 149- 164.

Risch, Marianne (1986): *Die Druckgraphik englischer Genremaler und die Düsseldorfer Malerschule 1820- 1850.* Diss. Univ. Kiel.

3.1.2.3 Regionale Malerei /Regional painting

3.1.2.3.1 Norddeutschland / Northern Germany

Claassen, Uwe (1996): *Fischernetz, Tracht und Bauernstube. Imaginiertes Landleben in norddeutscher Malerei des 19. Jahrhunderts. (Studien zur*

Volkskunde und Kulturgeschichte Schleswig-Holsteins, Bd. 33). Neumünster: Wachholtz.

Freunde der Hamburger Kunsthalle (Hrsg.) (1996): *Mit klarem Blick. Hamburger Malerei im Biedermeier.* (Ausst.-Kat.) Hamburg [u.a.]: Junius-Verlag.

Kaufmann, Gerhard (Hrsg.) (1973): *Volkslebenbilder aus Norddeutschland.* (Ausst.-Kat.) Hamburg: Altonaer Museum.

Scheele, Friedrich (Hrsg.) (1998): *Arbeitsalltag an der Nordseeküste: in Bildern von Bernhard Suerdieck, Adolf Fischer-Gurig und Max Liebermann. Zur gleichnamigen Ausstellung im Ostfriesischen Landesmuseum Emden vom 1. Februar bis 29. März 1998. (Ostfriesisches Landesmuseum und Emder Rüstkammer: Veröffentlichungen des Ostfriesischen Landesmuseums und Emder Rüstkammer; H. 2).* Oldenburg: Isensee.

3.1.2.3.2 Rhein-Main Gebiet / Rhine-Main area

Großkinsky, Manfred (Hrsg.) (2004): *Bilder aus dem Leben. Genremalerei im Rhein-Main-Gebiet.* (Ausst.-Kat.) Frankfurt am Main.

Landschulz, Marlene (1977): *Mainzer Maler aus der ersten Hälfte des 19. Jahrhunderts. Die Meister und ihre Werke.* Diss. phil. Univ. Mainz.

Trier, Eduard/ Weyres, Willy (Hrsg.) (1979): *Kunst des 19. Jahrhunderts im Rheinland. Band 3: Malerei.* Düsseldorf: Schwann.

3.1.2.3.3 Süddeutschland / Southern Germany

Balogh, László (1989): *Alltagsschilderung in der Münchner Malerei.* Mainburg: Pinsker.

Ebertshäuser, Heidi (1979): *Malerei im 19. Jahrhundert: Münchner Schule: Gesamtdarst. u. Künstlerlexikon.* München: Keyser.

Eiermann, Wolf (Hrsg.) (2001): *Württemberg. Maler entdecken Land und Leute; 1750- 1900.* (Ausst.-Kat.) Stuttgart: Theiss/ Stuttgart: Staatsgalerie.

Heimatmuseum Reutlingen (Hrsg.) (2007): *Württembergs Künstlerkolonie. Genremaler im Trachtendorf Betzingen.* (Ausst.-Kat.) Reutlingen: Stadtverwaltung.

Heyn, Hans (1980): *Süddeutsche Malerei aus dem bayerischen Hochland: d. Inntal, d. Chiemgau u. d. Berchtesgadner Land in bildner. Zeugnissen.* Rosenheim: Rosenheimer Verlagshaus.

Hofstätter, Hans H. (Hrsg.) (1986): *Das Schwarzwaldbild.* Freiburg i. Br.: Schillinger.

Rochard, Patricia (Hrsg.) (1996): *Mensch und Natur. Schwäbische Malerei im 19. Jahrhundert.* (Ausst.-Kat.) Mainz: Schmidt.

Scharfe, Martin (Hrsg.) (1983): *Heitere Gefühle bei der Ankunft auf dem Lande. Bilder schwäbischen Landlebens im 19. Jh.* (Ausst.-Kat.) Tübingen: Tübinger Vereinigung für Volkskunde.

Schlossmuseum d. Marktes Murnau (Hrsg.) (2006): *„Damals in Oberbayern". Land und Leute im 19. Jahrhundert.* (Ausst.-Kat.) Murnau: Schlossmuseum Murnau.

Wynen, Arnulf M./ Pfeiffer, Andreas (1981): *Volksleben in Baden und Württemberg. Gesehen mit Künstleraugen d. 19. Jh.* (Ausst.-Kat.) Heilbronn: Städt. Museen.

3.1.2.4 Spezielle Themenbereiche / Specific subject areas

Andresen, Wibke (1987): *Die Darstellung des städtischen Lebens in der deutschen Malerei des späten 19. Jahrhunderts. (Tuduv-Studien, Reihe Kunstgeschichte, Bd. 26).* München: tuduv-Verl.-Ges.

Andrian-Werburg, Bettina von (1990): *Schwälmer Arbeitswelt in der Sicht Willingshäuser Künstler des 19. und frühen 20. Jahrhunderts. Ideologiekritische Studien zur volkskundlichen Bildquellenforschung.* Diss. Univ. Marburg.

Bertuleit, Sigrid (2006): *Eine Stunde in der Ausstellung: Kinder! Bildnisse und Genreszenen. Rundgang in 2 x 12 Bildern.* (Ausst.-Kat.) Schweinfurt: Museum Georg Schäfer.

Lukatis, Christiane (1995): *Mein blauer Salon. Zimmerbilder der Biedermeierzeit.* (Ausst.-Kat.) Nürnberg: Germanisches Nationalmuseum.

May, Elisabeth (2000): *Jung und Alt im Spiegel bürgerlicher Imagination. Bauernromantik und Alltagsidylle in der Malerei des letzten Drittels des 19. Jahrhunderts. (Europäische Hochschulschriften: Reihe 28, Kunstgeschichte, Bd. 356).* Frankfurt am Main [u.a.]: Lang.

Muhr, Stefanie (2006): *Der Effekt des Realen. Die historische Genremalerei des 19. Jahrhunderts.* Köln [u.a.]: Böhlau.

Müller, Siegfried (1999): Der Dreißigjährige Krieg in der deutschen Historien- und Genremalerei des 19. Jahrhunderts, in: *Zeitschrift für Kunstgeschichte,* 62. Bd., Heft 1, S. 1- 27.

Schlapeit-Beck, Dagmar (1985): *Frauenarbeit in der Malerei 1870- 1900. Das Arbeitsbild im deutschen Naturalismus.* (Diss. Gesamthochschul. Wuppertal, 1984 u.d.T.: Die Darstellung von Frauenarbeit in der Malerei des deutschen Naturalismus) Berlin (West): Verl. für Ausbildung und Studium in der Elefanten Press.

Schmacke, Ernst (Hrsg.) (1994): *Industriebilder. Gemälde einer Epoche.* Münster: Ardey-Verl.

Sitt, Martina (1996): „In meinen Armen, in meinem Schoß". Die Darstellung der Mutterfigur in der Genremalerei des 17. und des 19. Jahrhunderts, in: *Verklärt, verkitscht, vergessen. Die Mutter als ästhetische Figur,* hrsg. von Renate Möhrmann, Stuttgart [u.a.]: Metzler, S. 145- 169.

3.1.3 Künstler / Artists

3.1.3.1 Ferdinand Brütt

Bastek, Alexander (2007): *Ferdinand Brütt und das städtisch-bürgerliche Genre um 1900.* (Diss. Univ. Hamburg, 2005) Weimar: VDG.

Museum Giersch, Frankfurt am Main (Hrsg.) (2007): *Ferdinand Brütt, 1849- 1936. Erzählung und Impression.* (Ausst.-Kat.) Petersberg: Imhof.

3.1.3.2 Heinrich Bürkel

Bühler, Hans-Peter/ Krückl, Albrecht (1989): *Heinrich Bürkel. Mit Werkverzeichnis der Gemälde*. München: Bruckmann.

Weber, Wilhelm (1969): Heinrich Bürkel – nicht nur ein „Genre-Maler", in: *Die Kunst und das schöne Heim. Monatsschr. für Malerei, Plastik, Graphik, Architektur u. Wohnkultur*, Bd. 81, S. 508- 510.

3.1.3.3 Franz Ludwig Catel

Bongaerts, Ursula (Hrsg.) (2007): *Der Landschafts- und Genremaler Franz Ludwig Catel (1778- 1856)*. (Ausst.-Kat.) Roma: Casa di Goethe; Bonn: AsKl.

Di Majo, Elena (Hrsg.) (1996): *Franz Ludwig Catel e i suoi amici a Roma. Un album di disegni dell'Ottocento*. (Ausst.-Kat.) Torino: Edizioni Sacs.

3.1.3.4 Johann Peter Hasenclever

Geppert, Stefan (Hrsg.) (2003): *Johann Peter Hasenclever (1810- 1853). Ein Malerleben zwischen Biedermeier und Revolution*. (Ausst.-Kat.) Main am Rhein: Philipp von Zabern.

Hütt, Wolfgang (1983): *Johann Peter Hasenclever*. Dresden: Verl. der Kunst.

Soiné, Knut (1990): *Johann Peter Hasenclever. Ein Maler im Vormärz. (Bergische Forschungen, Bd. 21)*. Neustadt/Aisch: Schmidt.

3.1.3.5 Carl Wilhelm Hübner

Landes, Lilian (2008): *Carl Wilhelm Hübner (1814- 1879). Genre und Zeitgeschichte im deutschen Vormärz. (Kunstwissenschaftliche Studien, Bd. 149)*. München [u.a.]: Dt. Kunstverlag.

Landes, Lilian (2011): Ästhetisierung des Sozialen im deutschen Vormärz. Carl Wilhelm Hübners sozialthematische Genremalerei, in: *Ästhetisierung des*

Sozialen. Reklame, Kunst und Politik im Zeitalter visueller Medien, hrsg. von Lutz Hieber und Stephan Moebius, Bielefeld: Transcript, S. 153- 176.

Stiftung Ostdeutsche Galerie (Hrsg.) (2001): *Carl Wilhelm Hübner. Abschied der Auswanderer, 1855. (Stiftung Ostdeutsche Galerie: Foyer-Ausstellung...; 9).* Regensburg: Stiftung Ostdeutsche Galerie.

3.1.3.6 Ludwig Knaus

Boekels, Ursula Mathilde (1999): *Die Genremalerei von Ludwig Knaus (1829- 1910): Das Frühwerk.* Diss. Univ. Bonn.

Gerz, Wolfgang (2000): Gesucht: Die Bäuerin von Rennerod. Der bekannte Genre-Maler Ludwig Knaus (1829- 1910) fand ein Modell im Westerwald, in: *Wäller Heimat. Jahrbuch des Westerwald-Kreises*, S. 134- 138.

Küster, Bernd (2001): *Ludwig Knaus, der Zeichner*. (Ausst.-Kat.) Gifkendorf: Merlin-Verl.

Schmidt, Heinz Ulrich (Hrsg.) (1979): *Ludwig Knaus, 1829- 1910.* Hanau: Peters.

3.1.3.7 Max Liebermann

Boskamp, Katrin (1994): *Studien zum Frühwerk von Max Liebermann. Mit einem Katalog der Gemälde und Ölstudien von 1866- 1889. (Studien zur Kunstgeschichte, Bd. 88).* Hildesheim/ Zürich [u.a.]: G. Olms.

Weber, Sylvia C. (Hrsg.) (2004): *Max Liebermann. Poesie des einfachen Lebens.* (Ausst.-Kat.) Wuppertal: Von-der-Heydt-Museum.

Wollers, Amke (2012): *Arbeitsdarstellungen im Frühwerk Max Liebermanns: Eine künstlerische Gratwanderung zwischen Realismus und Genre.* Magisterarbeit Univ. Kiel: Grin Verlag.

3.1.3.8 Adolph Menzel

Lammel, Gisold (1993): *Adolph Menzel. Bildwelt und Bildregie (Adolph Menzel, Bd. 1).* Dresden/Basel: Verlag der Kunst.

Lammel, Gisold (1993): *Adolph Menzel und seine Kreise (Adolph Menzel, Bd. 2).* Dresden/Basel: Verlag der Kunst.

3.1.3.9 Moritz Daniel Oppenheim

Graf, Esther (2004): *Die jüdische Genremalerei der voremanzipatorischen Zeit als Motivquelle für Moritz Daniel Oppenheims Zyklus zum altjüdischen Familienleben: Eine gattungs- und motivgeschichtliche Untersuchung.* Diss. Hochschule für Jüdische Studien Heidelberg.

Hufnagl-Brunner, Hilde (2001): *Jüdische Bildthematik im Genrewerk Moritz Daniel Oppenheims. Ein Beispiel motivischer Spezialisierung in der deutschen Genremalerei des 19. Jahrhunderts.* Dipl.-Arb. Univ. Wien.

3.1.3.10 Hubert Salentin

Neher, Mayme Frances Waltraut (1983): *Hubert Salentin: ein Vertreter des poetischen Genre in der Düsseldorfer Malerschule.* Diss. Univ. Bonn.

Neher, Mayme Frances Waltraut (1989): Hubert Salentin und sein poetisches Genre. Die Bedeutung der Genremalerei unter dem Akademiedirektor Friedrich Wilhelm von Schadow, dem Begründer der Düsseldorfer Malerschule, in: *Weltkunst. Zeitschrift für Kunst und Antiquitäten,* Bd. 59. S. 2744- 2748.

Neher, Mayme Frances Waltraut (2008*): Hubert Salentin. 1822 Zülpich – 1910 Düsseldorf. Der Poet in der Düsseldorfer Malerschule, Meisterschüler von Friedrich Wilhelm von Schadow.* Köln: Hanstein.

3.1.3.11 Theodor Schütz

Hipp, Elisabeth/ Becker, Jörg/ Eiermann, Wolf (2000): *Theodor Schüz: 1830- 1900 [anlässlich der Ausstellung im Stadtmuseum Tübingen (Genrebilder, Portraits und Illustrationen) und in der Städtischen Galerie Albstadt (Landschaften und Bilder ländlichen Lebens) 16. April- 2. Juli 2000].* (Ausst.-Kat.) Albstadt: Richard Conzelmann Grafik + Druck.

Oehler, Hans Albrecht/ Röben, Martina (1996): *Theodor Schüz. Schwäbischer Genremaler.* Grafenau: Ed. Schlichtenmaier.

3.1.3.12 Reinhard Sebastian Zimmermann

Coseriu, Maren (1984): Der Genremaler Reinhard Sebastian Zimmermann. Ein Hagnauer wurde in München berühmt, in: *Leben am See. Das Jahrbuch des Bodenseekreises*, Bd. 2, S. 192- 198.

Coseriu, Maren/ Tann, Siegfried (Hrsg.) (1986): *R. S. Zimmermann. Der Genremaler Reinhard Sebastian Zimmermann, 1815- 1893.* (Ausst.-Kat.) Friedrichshafen: Gessler.

3.1.3.13 Sonstige / Others

Articus, Rüdiger (1994): *Christian Ludwig Bokelmann. Ein wiederentdeckter Volkslebenmaler des 19. Jahrhunderts.* (Ausst.-Kat.) Hamburg: Hamburger Museum für Archäologie und der Geschichte Harburgs, Helms-Museum.

Ballmann, Bernd (1997): Kaspar Kaltenmoser. Ein Horber Genremaler der Münchner Schule, in: *Horb am Neckar. Natur und Geschichte erleben*, hrsg. von Joachim Lipp, Horb a.N.: Kultur- u. Museumsverein, S. 317- 324.

Ballmann, Bernd (2003): Salomon Hirschfelder, 1831- 1903. Ein Genremaler aus Dettensee, in: *Schwäbische Heimat. Zeitschrift für Regionalgeschichte, württembergische Landeskultur, Naturschutz und Denkmalpflege*, Bd. 54, S. 139- 150.

Balogh, László (1991): *Eduard von Grützner: 1846- 1925. Ein Münchner Genremaler der Gründerzeit. Monographie und kritisches Verzeichnis seiner Ölgemälde, Ölstudien und Ölskizzen.* Mainburg: Pinsker.

Baumann, Bringfriede (1986): *Der Münchner Maler Wilhelm Marc (1839- 1907). Monographie u. Werkverz. (Miscellanea Bavarica Monacensia, Bd. 139. Neue Schriftenreihe des Stadtarchivs München).* München: Uni-Druck.

Baumstark, Brigitte/ Bieber, Sylvia/ Baumgärtel, Bettina (Hrsg.) (2009): *Adolph Schroedter: Humor und Poesie im Biedermeier.* (Ausst.-Kat.) Karlsruhe: Städtische Galerie Karlsruhe.

Berger-Fix, Andrea (1996): *Friedrich Keller. Ein schwäbischer Realist.* (Ausst.-Kat.) Ludwigsburg.

Berndal, Franz (1968): Der Berliner Genremaler Curt Agthe, in: *Mitteilungen des Vereins für die Geschichte Berlins,* Jg. 64, S. 169- 171.

Bose, Herbert von (2007): *Das Bild des Fremden im Werk von Ludwig Emil Grimm (1790- 1863).* (Diss. Univ. Tübingen, 2004) Marburg: Tectum-Verl.

Brosch, Helmut (1980): Wilhelm Emelé. 1830- 1905. Leben und Werk, in: *700 Jahre Stadt Buchen. Beiträge zur Stadtgeschichte,* hrsg. von Rainer Trunk, Helmut Brosch und Karl Lehrer. Buchen/Odenwald: Bürgermeisteramt, S. 245- 258.

Brosch, Helmut (2005): *Wilhelm Emelé (1830- 1905), Historien- und Genremaler: er malte für Kaiser und Könige...* (Ausst.-Kat.) Buchen: Verein Bezirksmuseum Buchen.

Brugger, Gabriele (Hrsg.) (2004): *Lebensweisen. Genremalerei von J. B. Kirner und J. B. Pflug.* (Ausst.-Kat.) Beuron: Beuroner Kunstverlag.

Eismann, Ingeborg (2001): August von der Embde. Ein Kasseler Porträt- und Genremaler, in: *Weltkunst. Zeitschrift für Kunst und Antiquitäten,* Bd. 71, S. 608- 609.

Hase-Schmundt, Ulrike von (2011): Ernst Wilhelm Rietschel (1824- 1860). Der Bildnis- und Genremaler, in: *Neues lausitzisches Magazin. Zeitschrift der oberlausitzischen Gesellschaft der Wissenschaften, Neue Folge,* Bd. 14, S. 61- 86.

Herfurth-Ruhr, Vanessa (1997): *Der Genremaler Heinz Heim. Ausgewählte Ölbilder aus den Sammlungen der Stadt Darmstadt. (2 Bände).* Magisterarbeit Univ. Frankfurt am Main.

Hümme, Julia (2007): *Gregor von Bochmann (1850- 1930): Leben und Werk eines deutschbaltischen Malers in Düsseldorf. (Bau + Kunst, Bd. 12).* Kiel: Verlag Ludwig.

Jensen, Jens Christian (2007): *Carl Spitzweg: 1808- 1885. (Pegasus-Bibliothek).* München [u.a.]: Prestel.

Lahmann, Marina (2004): Pferde, Genre und Soldaten – der Maler Reinhold Braun. 1821 Altensteig – 1884 München, in: *Der Landkreis Calw. Ein Jahrbuch,* Bd. 22, S. 51- 66.

Ludwig, Horst (1979): Differenzierte Farbigkeit in volkstümlicher Genremalerei. Wilhelm von Diez und seine Schule, in: *Weltkunst. Zeitschrift für Kunst und Antiquitäten,* Bd. 49, S. 2540- 2542.

Mildenberger, Hermann (1984): Johann Baptist Seele. Genreszenen aus der Zeit um 1800, in: *Schwäbische Heimat. Zeitschrift für Regionalgeschichte, württembergische Landeskultur, Naturschutz und Denkmalpflege,* Bd. 35, S. 339- 349.

Munack, Wiltrud (2005): *Der Regensburger Maler Hans Kranzberger (1804- 1850). Monographie und Werkverzeichnis.* (Ausst.-Kat.) Regensburg: Univ.-Verl. Regensburg.

Müller, Karlernst (2002): *Die Brüder und Genremaler Julius und Otto Günther.* Ottweiler.

Nagel, Günter (1997): Adolf Werner – ein fast unbekannter Porträt- und Genremaler der Niederlausitz, in: *Niederlausitzer Studien,* Bd. 28, S. 43- 53.

Paluch, Luise (1983): *Lorenzo Quaglio: 1793- 1869. (Oberbayerisches Archiv, 108).* München: Verl. des Histor. Vereins von Oberbayern.

Reinhardt, Brigitte (1977): *Der Münchner Schlachten- und Genremaler Peter von Heß. (Oberbayerisches Archiv, 102).* München: Verlag des Historischen Vereins von Oberbayern.

Rösch, Rudolf (2010): *Der Maler Ferdinand von Piloty der Jüngere. Analyse seiner Werke bezüglich Thematik und Gestaltung vor dem Hintergrund der kulturellen, gesellschaftlichen und politischen Verhältnisse in Bayern*. Diss. Univ. Salzburg.

Scheible-Schober, Petra/ Helmbrecht, Jürgen (1996): *Jakob Grünenwald: 1821- 1896. Ein schwäbischer Genremaler. (Veröffentlichungen des Stadtarchivs Göppingen, 35)*. Weissenhorn: Konrad.

Scheible-Schober, Petra (1998): Jakob Grünenwald. Ein Schwabe in Bayern; in: *Weltkunst. Zeitschrift für Kunst und Antiquitäten*, Bd. 68, Nr. 6, S. 1207- 1209.

Schlink, Wilhelm (1972): Friedrich Wasmann als Genremaler. Über ein neuaufgefundenes Bild im Behnhaus zu Lübeck, in: *Wallraf-Richartz-Jahrbuch. Jahrbuch für Kunstgeschichte*, Bd. 34, S. 369- 378.

Spies, Gerd (1988): *Vom Leben braunschweigischer Landleute. Volkslebenbilder von Carl Schröder (1802- 1867). Ausstellung im Städtischen Museum am Löwenwall.* (Ausst.-Kat.) Braunschweig: Städtisches Museum.

Stapf, Peter (2010): Poesie der Alltäglichkeit. Max Thedy und die Herausbildung einer Genre- und Interieurmalerei in der Nachfolge der niederländischen Malerei, in: *Hinaus in die Natur! Barbizon, die Weimarer Malerschule und der Aufbruch zum Impressionismus*, hrsg. von Gerda Wendermann, Bielefeld: Kerber, S. 213- 217.

Wappenschmidt, Toni (1990): Die reine Welt der Kindheit. Der Düsseldorfer Genremaler Hugo Oehmichen, in: *Weltkunst. Zeitschrift für Kunst und Antiquitäten*, Bd. 60, S. 3040- 3043.

Wolfson, Michael (1990): Kerstings „Caspar David Friedrich im Atelier" und die Wiederentdeckung der holländischen Genremalerei, in: *Niederdeutsche Beiträge zur Kunstgeschichte*, Bd. 29, S. 202- 210.

3.2 Frankreich / France

3.2.1 Malerei des 19. Jahrhunderts / 19th century painting

Allard, Sébastien/ Loyrette, Henri (2007): *Nineteenth century French art. Art francais. From Romanticism to Impressionism, post-impressionism and Art Nouveau.* Paris: Flammarion.

Meixner, Laura L. (1995): *French realist painting and the critique of American society, 1865- 1900.* Cambridge/ New York: Cambridge University Press.

Weisberg, Gabriel P. (1980): *The realist tradition: French painting and drawing, 1830- 1900.* Cleveland: Cleveland Museum of Art/ Bloomington, Ind.: distributed by Indiana University Press.

3.2.2 Genremalerei / Genre painting

Blumenfeld, Carole (2011): *Petits théâtres de l'intime: la peinture de genre francaise entre Révolution et Restauration.* (Ausst.-Kat.) Toulouse: Musée des Augustins.

Costamagna, Philippe (2008): *La peinture de genre au temps du cardinal Fesch. Actes du colloque, Ajaccio, 15 juin 2007.* Paris: Gourcuff Gradenigo [u.a.].

Fehl, Rebekka (1999): *Der Bauer und die Avantgarde. Die Darstellung des Landmannes in der französischen Malerei des 19. Jahrhunderts. (Punctum 13).* München: scaneg.

Gotlieb, Marc J. (1991): *From genre to decoration. Studies in the theory and criticism of French salon painting, 1850- 1900.* (Diss. (Ph.D.) The Johns Hopkins University). Baltimore Md: The Johns Hopkins University.

Green, Anna (2007): *French paintings of childhood and adolescence: 1848- 1886.* Aldershot [u.a.]: Ashgate.

Howat, Rachel Jane (2005): *In what sense do genre paintings represent 'modern life'?.* Thesis (M.A.) Univ. of London.

Juneja, Monica (1998): *Peindre le paysan. L'image rurale dans la peinture francaise de Millet à Van Gogh.* Paris: Ed. du Makar.

Marlet, Jean Henri (1980): *Pariser Volksleben. Nach d. kolorierten Lithogr. d. „Tableaux de Paris". (Die bibliophilen Taschenbücher, 182).* Dortmund: Harenberg-Lexikon-Verl.

Rogers, Anne Trouillet (2005): *Ennui en plein air: Re-examining leisure and the flâneur in selected French genre painting.* Thesis (M.A.), Univ. of London, (Courtauld Institute of Art).

Schumacher, Ulrich (1979): Gruppenportrait und Genrebild. Zur Bedeutung der Photographie für die französische Malerei des 19. Jahrhunderts, in: *Giessener Beiträge zur Kunstgeschichte,* Bd. 4, S. 19- 61.

Sterling and Francine Clark Art Institute (Hrsg.) (1974): *The Elegant academics: chroniclers of nineteenth-century Parisian life.* (Ausst.-Kat.) North Adams, Mass.: Printed by Lamb Print. Co.

Zafran, Eric M. (1992): *Cavaliers and cardinals. Nineteenth-century French anecdotal paintings.* (Ausst.-Kat.) Cincinnati, Ohio: Taft Museum.

Zanella, Andrea (2007): La peinture de genre en France entre la Révolution et l'Empire, in: *Le cardinal Fesch et l'art de son temps. Fragonard, Marguerite Gérard, Jacques Sablet, Louis-Léopold Boilly...;* hrsg. von Philippe Costamagna und Carole Blumenfeld. Paris: Gallimard, S. 132- 169.

3.2.3 Künstler / Artists

3.2.3.1 Louis-Leopold Boilly

Eliel, Carol S. (1985): *Form and content in the genre works of Louis- Leopold Boilly.* Diss. (Ph.D.) Univ. New York.

Hallam, John Stephen (1981): The two manners of Louis-Léopold Boilly and French genre painting in transition, in: *The art bulletin. A quarterly publ. by the College Art Association of America,* Bd. 63, S. 618- 633.

Hallam, John Stephen (1984): *The genre works of Louis-Léopold Boilly.* (Diss. phil. Univ. of Washington, 1979) Ann Arbor: UMI.

Siegfried, Susan L. (1989): Boilly's "Moving House":"An Exact Picture of Paris"?; in: *Art Institute of Chicago Museum Studies,* Bd. 15, Nr. 2, S. 126- 137, 175- 177.

Siegfried, Susan L. (1995): *The art of Louis-Léopold Boilly. Modern life in Napoleonic France.* New Haven [u.a.]: Yale University Press.

3.2.3.2 Jules Breton

Bourrut Lacouture, Annette (2002): *Jules Breton. La chanson des blés.* (Ausst.-Kat.) Paris: Somogy [etc.].

Sturges, Hollister (1982): *Jules Breton and the French rural tradition.* Omaha, Nebr. [u.a.]: Joslyn Art Museum [u.a.].

3.2.3.3 Ernest Meissonier

Gotlieb, Marc J. (1996): *The plight of emulation. Ernest Meissonier and French salon painting. (The Princeton series in nineteenth-century art, culture, and society).* Princeton, NJ: Princeton University Press.

Hungerford, Constance Cain (1999): *Ernest Meissonier. Master in his genre.* Cambridge [u.a.]: Cambridge University Press.

3.2.3.4 Jean-Francois Millet

Fermigier, André (1979): *Jean-Francois Millet.* Stuttgart: Klett-Cotta.

Meixner, Laura L. (1983): Popular Criticism of Jean-Francois Millet in Nineteenth-Century America, in: *The Art Bulletin,* Bd. 65, Nr. 1, S. 94- 105.

Shackelford, George T. M./ Goldin, Marco (Hrsg.) (2005): *Millet. Sessanta capolavori dal Museum of Fine Arts di Boston.* (Ausst.-Kat.) Conegliano: Linea d'ombra.

3.2.3.5 Sonstige / Others

Bänteli, Timea (2011): *William Adolphe Bouguereaus Genremalerei und die französische Kunst des 19. Jahrhunderts.* Lic. phil. I Univ. Zürich.

Blumenfeld, Carole (2011): *Marguerite Gérard et la peinture de genre de la fin des années 1770 aux années 1820.* (2 vol.). Diss. Histoire de l'art, Lille 3.

Chesneau-Dupin, Laurence/ Caffort, Michel (Hrsg.) (2000): *Jean-Victor Schnetz, 1787- 1870: couleurs d'Italie.* Flers: Musée du Château de Flers/ Cabourg, France: Éditions Cahiers du temps.

Dunifer, Vada (1985): Two veterans playing ‚Piquet'. A genre painting with disguised political content, in: *Konsthistorisk tidskrift. Journal of art history. Art review*, Bd. 54, S. 170- 180.

Papounaud, Benoît-Henry (Hrsg.) (2004): *Edouard Onslow. Un peintre en Auvergne au XIXe siècle.* (Ausst.-Kat.) Clermont-Ferrand: Un, Deux ... Quatre Éd.

Volkmar, Karl Franklin (1989): *Camille Pissarro's "Jardiniere" (1884- 1885) in the context of his early "genre" paintings: 1872- 1886.* (Diss. (Ph.D.) The Ohio State University, 1985). Ann Arbor, MI: University Microfilms International.

Zanella, Andrea (2004): *Jean-Baptiste Mallet, peintre grassois: Grasse, Musée de la Parfumerie Fragonard, 4 Juin- 4 Septembre 2004.* Grasse: Fragonard.

3.3 Griechenland / Greece

Didaskalu, Kōnstantinos (1991): *Genre- und allegorische Malerei von Nikolaus Gysis.* Diss. Univ. München.

Katsanaki, Maria (2007): *Le peintre Théodore Ralli (1852- 1909) et son oeuvre.* Diss. Univ. Paris.

Lydakis, Stelios (1972): *Geschichte der griechischen Malerei des 19. Jahrhunderts. (Materialien zur Kunst des neunzehnten Jahrhunderts, Bd. 7).* München: Prestel-Verlag.

3.4 Großbritannien / Great Britain

3.4.1 England / England

3.4.1.1 Malerei des 19. Jahrhunderts / 19th century painting

Herrmann, Luke John (2000): *Nineteenth century British painting.* London: De la Mare.

Lambourne, Lionel (1999): *Victorian painting.* London: Phaidon.

Paxman, Jeremy (2009): *The Victorians. Britain through the paintings of the age.* London: BBC.

Treuherz, Julian (1993): *Victorian painting.* New York: Thames and Hudson.

Valentine, Helen (1999): *Art in the age of Queen Victoria: treasures from the Royal Academy of Arts permanent collection.* London: Royal Academy of Arts in association with Yale University Press, New Haven and London.

Warner, Malcolm (Hrsg.) (1997): *The Victorians. British painting 1837- 1901.* (Ausst.-Kat.) New York: Abrams.

3.4.1.2 Genremalerei / Genre painting

3.4.1.2.1 Überblick / General works

Bennett, Shelley M. (1985): *British narrative drawings and watercolors, 1660- 1880: twenty-two examples from the Huntington collection.* San Marino, Calif.: Huntington Library.

Casteras, Susan P. (1999): *The defining moment: Victorian narrative paintings from the Forbes Magazine Collection.* Charlotte, N.C.: Mint Museum of Art.

Christopher Wood Gallery (Hrsg.) (1990): *People and rooms: spring exhibition of Victorian narrative pictures and interiors.* (Ausst.-Kat.) London: Christopher Wood Gallery.

Cowling, Mary (2000): *Victorian figurative painting. Domestic life and the contemporary social scene.* Windsor: Andreas Papadakis.

Green, Richard (1979): *The Victorian Scene.* London: Richard Green Gallery.

Hadfield, John (1985): *Every picture tells a story: images of Victorian life*. New York, N.Y.: Facts on File Publications.

Johnson, Edward Dudley Hume (1986): *Paintings of the British social scene. From Hogarth to Sickert*. New York: Rizzoli.

Jura, Martina (1985): *Rahmenmotive in der englischen Genremalerei des 19. Jahrhunderts*. Diss. Techn. Hochschule Aachen.

Lambourne, Lionel (1982): *An introduction to 'Victorian' genre painting from Wilkie to Frith*. London: Her Majesty's Stationary Office.

Lister, Raymond (1966): *Victorian narrative paintings*. New York: Potter.

Mount, Harry Thomas (1991): *The reception of Dutch genre painting in England 1695- 1829*. Diss. Univ. of Cambridge.

Sartin, Stephen (1978): *A dictionary of British narrative painters*. Leigh-on-Sea: F. Lewis.

Sitwell, Sacheverell (1969): *Narrative pictures. A survey of English genre and its painters*. London: Batsford.

Solkin, David H. (2008): *Painting out of the ordinary. Modernity and the art of everyday life in early nineteenth-century Britain*. New Haven, Conn. [u.a.]: Yale University Press.

Thomas, Julia (2000): *Victorian narrative painting*. London: Tate Publishing.

Valentine, Helen (Hrsg.) (2008): *From all walks of life: genre paintings from the Royal Academy Collection: an introduction to the display*. London: Royal Academy of Arts.

Wood, Christopher (1990): *Victorian panorama. Paintings of Victorian life*. London: Faber and Faber.

3.4.1.2.2 Spezielle Themenbereiche / Specific subject areas

Anderson, Gail-Nina/ Wright, Joanne (Hrsg.) (1997): *The pursuit of leisure. Victorian depictions of pastimes*. (Ausst.-Kat.) London: Lund Humphries.

Casteras, Susan P. (1986): *Victorian childhood: paintings selected from the Forbes Magazine collection by Christopher Forbes*. (Ausst.-Kat.) New York: Abrams.

Dewing, David (Hrsg.) (2003): *Home and garden. Paintings and drawings of English, middle-class, urban domestic spaces 1675 to 1914.* (Ausst.-Kat.) London: Geffrye Museum Publ.

Edelstein, T.J. (1979): *"But who shall paint the griefs of those oppress'd?": the social theme in Victorian painting.* Diss. Univ. of Pennsylvania.

Fletcher, P. (2009): "To wipe a manly tear": The Aesthetics of Emotion in Victorian Narrative Painting; in: *Victorian studies*, Bd. 51, Nr. 3, S. 457- 469.

Marshall, Nancy Rose (2012): *City of gold and mud. Painting Victorian London.* New Haven, Conn. [u.a.]: Yale University Press.

Payne, Christiana (1998): *Rustic simplicity. Scenes of cottage life in nineteenth-century British art.* (Ausst.-Kat.) Nottingham.

Prettejohn, Elizabeth (1996): Recreating Rome in Victorian Painting. From history to genre, in: *Imagining Rome. British artists and Rome in the nineteenth century,* hrsg. von Michael Liversidge und Catharine Edwards, London: Merrell Holberton, S. 54- 69.

Rodee, Howard D. (1977): The "Dreary Landscape" as a Background for Scenes of Rural Poverty in Victorian Paintings; in: *Art Journal,* Bd. 36, Nr. 4, S. 307- 313.

Thomas, Julia (2004): *Pictorial Victorians: the inscription of values in word and image.* Athens: Ohio University Press.

Treuherz, Julian (1987): *Hard times: social realism in Victorian art.* (Ausst.-Kat.) London: Lund Humphries in association with Manchester City Art Gallery.

Wood, Christopher (1988): *Paradise lost: paintings of English country life and landscape 1850- 1914.* London: Barrie & Jenkins.

3.4.1.3 Künstler / Artists

3.4.1.3.1 William Powell Frith

Bills, Mark (2004): William Powell Frith's 'The Crossing Sweeper': An Archetypal Image of Mid-Nineteenth-Century London, in: *The Burlington Magazine,* Bd. 146, Nr. 1214 (British Art), S. 300- 307.

Bills, Mark/ Knight, Vivien (Hrsg.) (2007): *William Powell Frith. Painting the Victorian age.* (Ausst.-Kat.) New Haven, Conn. [u.a.]: Yale University Press.

Noakes, Aubrey (1978): *William Frith. Extraordinary Victorian painter. A biographical and critical essay.* London: Jupiter.

Wood, Christopher (2006): *William Powell Frith: A painter & his world.* Stroud [England]: Sutton Publishing.

3.4.1.3.2 Sonstige / Others

Allwood, Rosamond (Hrsg.) (1982): *George Elgar Hicks. Painter of Victorian life. Geffrye Museum, London, 1.10.1982- 3.1.1983; Southampton Art Gallery, 17.1.- 22.2.1983.* London: Inner London Education Authority.

Bills, Mark (2002): 'The General Post Office – one minute to six' by George Elgar Hicks, in: *The Burlington magazine*, Bd. 144, Nr. 1194, S. 550- 556.

Jenkins, Adrian (2000): *Painters and peasants. Henry LaThangue and British rural naturalism 1880- 1905.* Bolton.

Laycock, Kathleen Mary (2006): *Out of obscurity: the artist Jane Maria Bowkett (1837- 1891).* Thesis (M.A.) Univ. of Victoria.

Parker, Terry (1998): *Golden hours: the paintings of Arthur J. Elsley, 1860- 1952.* Somerset: Richard Dennis.

Roe, F. Gordon (1978): *Fred Roe, R.I. (1864- 1947). Historical and genre painter, author and antiquary, his life and art, with a catalogue of his works compiled by his son F. Gordon Roe F.S.A.*

Salveson, Magdalena A. (1968): *W. Collins and W. Mulready: the increase of child genre.* Thesis (M.A.) Univ. of London (Courtauld Institute of Art).

3.4.2 Schottland / Scotland

3.4.2.1 Überblick / General works

Errington, Lindsay (1980): *The artist and the kirk*. Edinburgh: The Gallery.

Forbes, Duncan (2000): ‚Dodging and watching the natural incidents of the peasantry': Genre painting in Scotland 1780- 1830, in: *The Oxford art journal*, Bd. 23, Nr. 2, S. 79- 94.

Macmillan, Duncan (2000): *Scottish art, 1460- 2000*. Edinburgh: Mainstream Pub.

3.4.2.2 Künstler / Artists

3.4.2.2.1 David Wilkie

Chiego, William J./ Miles, H.A.D./ Brown, David Blayney (1987): *Sir David Wilkie of Scotland (1785- 1841)*. Raleigh: North Carolina Museum of Art.

Errington, Lindsay (1985): *Tribute to Wilkie: From the National Gallery of Scotland, with contributions by Turner, Landseer, Frith and others*. (Ausst.-Kat.) Edinburgh: National Galleries of Scotland.

Irwin, Francina (1974): Wilkie at the Cross Roads, in: *The Burlington Magazine*, Bd. 116, Nr. 853, S. 212, 214- 216.

Mainhill Gallery/ Bourne Fine Art (Hrsg.) (1983): *The Wilkie tradition: An exhibition of Scottish genre paintings of the early 19th century*. (Ausst.-Kat.) St. Boswells: Edinburgh: Mainhill Gallery/ Bourne Fine Art.

McCurdy, Melinda Ruth (2005): *History and human experience in the art of David Wilkie, 1806- 1835*. Diss. (Ph.D.) University of California, Santa Barbara.

Pointon, Marcia (1984): From 'Blind Man's Buff' to 'Le Colin Maillard': Wilkie and His French Audience, in: *Oxford Art Journal*, Bd. 7, Nr. 1, S. 15- 25.

Tromans, Nicholas (Hrsg.) (2002): *David Wilkie. Painter of everyday life*. (Ausst.-Kat.) London: Dulwich Picture Gallery.

Tromans, Nicholas (2007): *David Wilkie. The people's painter*. Edinburgh: Edinburgh University Press.

3.5 Irland / Ireland

3.5.1 Überblick / General works

Aherne, Mark (1996): *Nineteenth-century Irish genre and sentimental painting.* Thesis (M.A.) Univ. College Dublin.

Crookshank, Anne/ Fitz-Gerald, Desmond John Viliers (2002): *Ireland's painters. 1600- 1940.* New Haven [u.a.]: Yale University Press.

Kinmonth, Claudia (2006): *Irish rural interiors in art.* New Haven, Conn.: Yale University Press.

3.5.2 Künstler / Artists

O'Byrne, Robert (2006): Success for Moynan's Genre Paintings, in: *Irish Arts Review,* Bd. 23, Nr. 4, S. 64.

O'Regan, Maebh (2006): Richard Moynan: Painting Privilege and Poverty, in: *Irish Arts Review,* Bd. 23, Nr. 4, S. 112- 117.

Pointon, Marcia R. (1986): *Mulready.* (Ausst.-Kat.) London: Victoria and Alberta Museum.

Salveson, Magdalena A. (1968): *W. Collins and W. Mulready: the increase of child genre.* Thesis (M.A.) Univ. of London (Courtauld Institute of Art).

3.6 Italien / Italy

3.6.1 Überblick / General works

Bietoletti, Silvestra (2007): La pittura di genere, in: *L'Ottocento in Italia. Le arti sorelle. Il realismo 1849- 1870*, hrsg. von Carlo Sisi, Milano: Mondadori, S. 89- 99.

Caretto, Patrizia (1993): *Aspetti di vita familiare e domestica nella pittura di genere ottocentesca. 104 opere d'autore*. (Ausst.-Kat.) Torino: Graf Art Ed.

Corradini, Mauro (1995): *La caccia nell'arte. L'illustrazione e la pittura di genere (La caccia nell'arte, Bd. 3)*. Firenze.

D'Amico, Antonio (Hrsg.) (2010): *Poesia d'interni. Angoli di vita nell'arte dell'800 italiano*. (Ausst.-Kat.) Milano: Bocca.

Galleria Aversa (Hrsg.) (1992): *Paesaggio e pittura di genere nell'800 e '900 italiano: proposte '92: dal 14 novembre al 20 dicembre 1992*. (Ausst.-Kat.) Torino: Galleria Aversa.

Gentili, Sandro/ Nardi, Isabella (Hrsg.) (2000): *L'immagine del quotidiano. Letteratura di costume e pittura di genere tra '700 e '800. (Incontri/ Università degli studi di Perugia, Letterature moderne e contemporanee, 9)*. Napoli [u.a.]: Edizioni Scientifiche Italiane.

Ginex, Giovanna (2005): "Pittura di genere". Lo sguardo sul popolo, in: *Pittura italiana nell'Ottocento.(Collana del Kunsthistorisches Institut in Florenz, Max Planck Institut, 9)*, hrsg. von Martina Hansmann, Venezia: Marsilio, S. 303-330.

Rizzoni, Gianni (Hrsg.) (1998): *Italia (com'era). Uomini, città e paesaggi nei dipinti del Settecento e dell'Ottocento*. Milano: Mondadori.

3.6.2 Regionale Malerei / Regional painting

3.6.2.1 Abruzzen / Abruzzo

Pierluigi, Silvan (Hrsg.) (2010): *Gente d'Abruzzo. Verismo sociale nella pittura abruzzese del XIX secolo*. (Ausst.-Kat.) Rom: Scienze e lettere.

3.6.2.2 Kampanien / Campania

Caputo, Rosario (Hrsg.) (1999): *L'Ottocento napoletano nelle collezioni private. Pitloo, Gigante, Palizzi, Morelli, De Gregorio, Rossano, Cammarano, Toma, Dalbono, Leto, De Nittis, Campriani, Michetti, Mancini, Migliaro*. Napoli: Grimaldi.

Gelao, Clara (Hrsg.) (2006): *Scene di vita popolare napoletana nei disegni, acquerelli, gouaches e litografie dell'archivio Congedo*. (Ausst.-Kat.) Galatina: Congedo.

3.6.2.3 Toskana / Tuscany

Baboni, Andrea (1994): *La pittura toscana dopo la macchia: 1865- 1920. L'evoluzione della pittura del vero: intrecci con la macchia e inizi del naturalismo, il vero tra pittura di genere, di storia e d'accademia*. Novara: Istituto geografico De Agostini.

3.6.2.4 Venetien und Lombardei / Veneto and Lombardy

Pirovano, Carlo (Hrsg.) (1998): *Luci e colori del vero. Genti e paesi nella pittura veneta e lombarda dalle collezione Ambroveneto, Banca Intesa e Fondazione Cariplo*. (Ausst.-Kat.) Milano: Electa.

Savoia, Enzo (Hrsg.) (2010): *Vita a Venezia. Colore e sentimento nella pittura veneta dell'800*. Milano: Bottegantica.

3.6.3 Künstler / Artists

3.6.3.1 Domenico Induno

Agliati Ruggia, Mariangela/ Rebora, Sergio (Hrsg.) (2002): *Intorno agli Induno. Pittura e scultura tra genere e storia nel Canton Ticino*. (Ausst.-Kat.) Milano: Skira.

Bietoletti, Silvestra (1991): *Domenico Induno. (Mensili d'arte, 10)*. Soncino: Edizioni dei Soncino.

Enrico, Franco (Hrsg.) (1996): *Pane e lagrime: un capolavoro ritrovato di Domenico Induno, 1815- 1878*. (Ausst.-Kat.) Milano: Enrico, Gallerie d'arte.

3.6.3.2 Sonstige / Others

Casprini, Federica (2005): *Carlo Iozzi (1844- 1929): Dall'accademia alla pittura di genere*. (Ausst.-Kat.) Firenze: Centro Di.

Di Giacomo, Domenico (2006): *Vincenzo Migliaro: 1858- 1938. Il pittore di Napoli*. Pescara: Ianeri Editore.

Marini, Giuseppe Luigi (2002): *Giovanni Battista Quadrone*. (Ausst.-Kat.) Torino: Ed. GAM.

Mazzocca, Fernando (Hrsg.) (1998): *Angelo Inganni: 1807-1880. Un pittore bresciano nella Milano romantica*. (Ausst.-Kat.) Milano: Skira.

Segramora, Paola (1993/94): *Veduta, cronaca urbana e pittura di genere nell'opera di Angelo Inganni*. (Diss. Univ. Milano) Milano: Università degli studi.

Serafini, Paolo (Hrsg.) (2010): *Giacomo Favretto. Venezia, fascino e seduzione*. Cinisello Balsamo (Milano): Silvana Ed.

Wassibauer, Thomas (2005): *Eugen von Blaas, 1843- 1931. Das Werk; catalogue raisonné; Skizzen, Aquarelle, Gemälde*. Hildesheim: Olms.

3.7 Niederlande / Netherlands

Dekker, J.J.H. (2003): Family on the Beach: Representations of Romantic and Bourgeois Family Values by Realistic Genre Painting of Nineteenth-Century Scheveningen Beach, in: *Journal of family history: studies in family, kinship and demography,* Bd. 28, Nr. 2, S. 277- 296.

Dekkers, Dieuwertje (1999): *Jozef Israe" ls, 1824- 1911.* (Ausst.-Kat.) Zwolle: Uitgeverij Waanders.

3.8 Polen / Poland

Blak, Halina/ Małkiewicz, Barbara/ Wojtałowa, Elżbieta (2001): *Polish painting of the 19th century (Modern Polish painting: the catalogue of collections)*. Cracow: NM.

Bühler, Hans-Peter (1993): *Jäger, Kosaken und polnische Reiter. Josef von Brandt, Alfred von Wierusz-Kowalski, Franz Roubaud und der Münchner Polenkreis*. Hildesheim [u.a.]: G. Olms.

Gwiazdowskiej, Ewa (Hrsg.) (2007): *August Ludwig Most (1807- 1883). Pomorski artysta epoki Biedermeieru: pommerscher Künstler der Biedermeierzeit*. Szczecin: Muzeum Narodowe.

Jäschke, Maria Magdalena (2009): *Traditionalismus und Moderne in der polnischen Landschafts- und Genremalerei um 1900. Konservativismus und Progressivität im Spannungsfeld. Dargestellt am Beispiel ausgewählter Werke von Józef Chełmoński, Leon Wyczółkowski und Jan Stanisławski*. Magisterarbeit Univ. München.

3.9 Russland / Russia

3.9.1 Überblick / General works

Aigner, Carl/ Belgin, Tayfun/ Lenjaschin, Wladimir (2002): *Russland. Repin und die Realisten.* (Ausst.-Kat.) Bad Breisig: Palace Ed.

Belgin, Tayfun (Hrsg.) (2004): *Liebe, Tod und Leidenschaft. Geschichten aus dem Zarenreich.* (Ausst.-Kat.) Bad Breisig: Palace Ed.

Eickel, Nancy (Hrsg.) (1986): *Russia. The land, the people. Russian painting, 1850-1910. From the collections of the State Tretyakov Gallery, Moscow and the State Russian Museum, Leningrad.* (Ausst.-Kat.) Washington, D.C.: Smithsonian Inst. Traveling Exhibition Service [u.a.]. (Aus dem Russischen von Nicholas Berkoff)

Gray, Rosalind (1997): *Western influence on Russian genre painting 1820- 1870.* Diss. (D. Phil.) University of Oxford.

Gray, Rosalind Polly (2000): *Russian genre painting in the nineteenth century.* Oxford [u.a.]: Clarendon Press.

Jackson, David (2006): *The wanderers and critical realism in nineteenth- century Russian painting.* Manchester [u.a.]: Manchester University Press.

Leek, Peter (2005): *Russische Malerei.* Bournemouth: Parkstone. (Aus dem Englischen)

Nesterova, Elena (1996): *Die Wanderer. Die Meister des russischen Realismus. Zweite Hälfte des 19. bis Anfang des 20. Jahrhunderts.* Bournemouth: Parkstone-Verl. [u.a.]. (Aus dem Russischen)

Ottomeyer, Hans/ Heinz, Marianne/ Biedermann, Birgit (1999): *Russische Malerei der Biedermeierzeit. Meisterwerke aus der Tretjakow-Galerie Moskau im Dialog mit Gemälden der Neuen Galerie Kassel.* (Ausst.-Kat.) Eurasburg: Ed. Minerva.

Pospelov, Gleb G./ Zabrodina, Julija M. (Hrsg.) (1989): *Russian drawings. 18th to early 20th century. The life drawing, the still life, the landscape, the life sketch, the animal drawing, the genre sketch, the portrait.* Leningrad: Aurora Art Publ.

Sarabianov, Dmitri Vladimirovich (1990): *Russian art: from neoclassicism to the avant garde, 1800- 1917: painting – sculpture – architecture.* New York: H. N. Abrams.

3.9.2 Künstler / Artists

Alekseeva, Tat'jana V. (Hrsg.) (1985): *Wenezianow und seine Schule.* Leningrad: Aurora-Kunstverlag. (Aus dem Russischen übertragen von Boris Zwetkow)

Nesterova, Elena Vladimirovna (2006): *Leonid Ivanovich Solomatkin.* Sankt-Peterburg: Zolotoĭ vek: Khudozhnik Rossii.

Stephanowitz, Traugott (1974): *Alexej Gawrilowitsch Wenezianow. (Welt der Kunst).* Berlin: Hentschelverlag Kunst u. Gesellschaft.

3.10 Schweiz / Switzerland

3.10.1 Überblick / General works

Keller, Heinz (1964): *Winterthurer Historien- und Genremalerei des 19. Jahrhunderts.* (Ausst.-Kat.) Winterthur.

Klemm, Christian (Hrsg.) (1998): *Von Anker bis Zünd. Die Kunst im jungen Bundesstaat, 1848- 1900.* (Ausst.-Kat.) Zürich: Scheidegger & Spiess.

3.10.2 Künstler / Artists

3.10.2.1 Albert Anker

Bhattacharya-Stettler, Therese (1994): Ich machte, was ich konnte, aber die Flügel eines Spatzes sind nicht die eines Adlers. Albert Anker als Genremaler, in: *Kunst + Architektur in der Schweiz: K + A,* Bd. 45, Nr. 4, S. 361- 367.

Stuber, Martin/ Gerber-Visser, Gerrendina/ Messerli, Isabelle (Hrsg.) (2010): *Ländliche Gesellschaft und materielle Kultur bei Albert Anker (1831- 1910). (Berner Zeitschrift für Geschichte und Heimatkunde No 2 [2010]).* Bern: Kunstmuseum.

3.10.2.2 Raphael Ritz

Ruppen, Walter (1971): *Raphael Ritz, 1829- 1894. Leben und Werk. Ein Walliser Maler des 19. Jahrhunderts aus der Düsseldorfer Schule.* (Diss. Univ. Freiburg in der Schweiz). Vira: Dürr.

Ruppen, Walter (1994): Der Genremaler Raphael Ritz. Ein Rückblick anlässlich des hundertsten Todestages, in: *Kunst + Architektur in der Schweiz: K + A,* Bd. 45, Nr. 4, S. 368- 374.

3.10.2.3 Sonstige / Others

Fischer, Rainald (1972): Ludwig Vogel, "Kapuziner im Dorf". Ein nazarenisches Genrebild und seine Vorstudien, in: *Unsere Kunstdenkmäler. Mitteilungsblatt für die Mitglieder der Gesellschaft für Schweizerische Kunstgeschichte*, Bd. 23, S. 161- 166.

Linxweiler, Karin (1996): *Ragamuffins. Frank Buchsers Genremalerei von schwarzen Amerikanern 1866- 1871*. (Lizentiatsarbeit, Institut für Kunstgeschichte, Univ. Bern). Bern: Universität.

3.11 Skandinavien / Scandinavia

3.11.1 Überblick / General works

Knopp, Katrin S. (2009): „… hier ist der starre gewaltige Norden." Skandinavische Landschafts- und Genremalerei im 19. Jahrhundert, in: *Facetten des Nordens. Räume – Konstruktionen – Identitäten*, hrsg. von Jan Hecker-Stampehl und Hendriette Kliemann-Geisinger. Berlin: Nordeuropa-Institut der Humboldt-Universität, S. 57- 92.

Ohlsen, Nils (1999): *Skandinavische Interieurmalerei zur Zeit Carl Larssons*. (Diss. Freie Univ. Berlin, 1998) Berlin: Reimer.

3.11.2 Dänemark / Denmark

Bonde Jensen, Jørgen (1993): *H.C. Andersen og genrebilledet*. København: Babette.

Juul Madsen, Preben (1988): *Danske genremalere. Fortællende billeder i 1800-tallet*. København: P. Fogtdal.

Mogensen, Margit (1984): *Landbruget i dansk malerkunst ca. 1840- 1915*. S.l.: Landbohistorisk selskab.

Zenius, Marianne (1976): *Genremaleri og virkelighed. En kildekritisk analyse over billeder af Chr. Dalsgaard, J. Exner og F. Vermehren*. København: Lokalhistorisk Afdeling.

3.11.3 Norwegen / Norway

Lange Marit (Hrsg.) (1996): *Harriet Backer: 1845- 1932*. (Ausst.-Kat.) Oslo: Nasjonalgalleriet.

Thue, Oscar (1997): *Christian Krohg*. Oslo: Aschehoug.

3.11.4 Schweden / Sweden

Bengtsson, Eva-Lena (1984/85): Amalia Lindegren: Aspects of a 19th-Century Artist, in: *Woman's Art Journal*, Bd. 5, Nr. 2, S. 16- 20.

Bengtsson, Eva-Lena (2000): *Verklighetens poesi. Svenska genrebilder 1825- 1880.* (Diss. Univ. Uppsala) Uppsala: Ubsaliensis Academiae.

3.12 Spanien / Spain

3.12.1 Überblick / General works

Cirici Narváez, Juan Ramón (2006): *La pintura costumbrista en el Museo de Cádiz.* (Ausst.-Kat.) Sevilla: Junta de Andalucía.

Díez, José Luis (Hrsg.) (2002): *Ternura y melodrama. Pintura de escenas familiares en tiempos de Sorolla. Museo del Siglo XIX, del 18 de diciembre de 2002 al 23 de febrero de 2003.* (Ausst.-Kat.) Valencia.

Sammer Gallery (Hrsg.) (1987): *Pintura de género del s. XIX: exposición.* Madrid/ Londres: Sammer Gallery.

3.12.2 Regionale Genremalerei / Regional genre painting

3.12.2.1 Andalusien / Andalusia

Quesada, Luis (1992): *La vida cotidiana en la pintura andaluza.* Sevilla: Focus, Fundación Fondo de Cultura de Sevilla.

Quesada, Luis (1996): *Pintores españoles y extranjeros en Andalucia.* Sevilla: Guadalquivir Ed.

Reina Palazón, Antonio (1979): *Pintura costumbrista en Sevilla (1830- 1870). (Publicaciones de la Universidad de Sevilla: Colección de bolsillo, Nr. 73).* Sevilla: Servicio de Publ. de la Univ. de Sevilla.

Torres Martín, Ramón (1980): *La pintura costumbrista sevillana.* (Ausst.-Kat.) Madrid: Club Urbis.

3.12.2.2 Kanarische Inseln / Canary Islands

Allen, Jonathan (Hrsg.) (2001): *Costumbre y realidad. Costumbrismo y realismo en la pintura canaria, 1860- 2000.* (Ausst.-Kat.) Las Palmas de Gran Canaria: La Caja de Canarias, Obra Social [u.a.].

3.12.3 Künstler / Artists

Barragán Jané, Montserrat/ Cano Rivero, Ignacio (Hrsg.) (2008): *Aguiar: otro costumbrismo: del 7 de noviembre de 2008 al 1 de marzo de 2009, Museo de Artes y Costumbres populares de Sevilla.* (Ausst.-Kat.) Sevilla: Junta de Andalucía, Consejería de Cultura.

Gea, Juan Carlos/ Masaveu, Pedro (2007): *Arte y vida cotidiana: exposición 2007: colección Masaveu. Lucas, Eugenio 1817- 1870.* Oviedo: Sociedad Anónima Tudela Veguín.

Johnston, William R. (1981): A contemporary genre painting by Raimundo de Madrazo y Garreta, in: *The journal of the Walters Art Gallery*, Bd. 33/34, S. 34- 41.

Páez Burruezo, Martín (2007): *Manuel Picolo López (1851- 1913): La pintura de género: Centro de Arte Palacio Almudí, 20 diciembre 2007- 30 enero 2008.* (Ausst.-Kat.) Murcia: Concejalía de Cultura.

Rubio Jiménez, Jesús (2008): *José María Domínguez Bécquer. (Arte hispalense, 82).* Sevilla: Deputación Provincial de Sevilla.

3.13 Ungarn / Hungary

Steinschneider, Nina (2008): *Menschenbilder. Die ungarische Genremalerei im 19. Jahrhundert.* Dipl.- Arb. Univ. Graz.

Supka, Magdolna B. (1974): *Genrebilder in der Ungarischen Nationalgalerie.* Budapest: Corvina Verl. (Aus dem Ungarischen übertragen von Zoltán Paulinyi.)

3.14 Österreich / Austria

3.14.1 Überblick / General works

Feuchtmüller, Rupert (1968): *Ausstellung: Alltag und Festbrauch im Biedermeier. Gemälde und Aquarelle aus den Sammlungen des Niederösterreichischen Landesmuseums, Wien.* Wien: Amt der Niederösterreichischen Landesregierung, Abt. III/2 (Kulturreferat).

Frodl, Gerbert/ Schröder, Klaus Albrecht (Hrsg.) (1992): *Wiener Biedermeier. Malerei zwischen Wiener Kongress und Revolution.* (Ausst.-Kat.) München: Prestel.

Grabner, Sabine (2006): *Mehr als Biedermeier. Klassizismus, Romantik und Realismus in der Österreichischen Galerie Belvedere.* München: Hirmer.

Kessler-Aurisch, Helga (1983): *Mode und Malerei in Wien. Vom Wiener Kongreß bis zum ersten Weltkrieg.* Diss. Univ. Freiburg (Breisgau).

Prokisch, Bernhard (Hrsg.) (1993): *Lebenswelten – Alltagsbilder.* (Ausst.-Kat.) Linz: Landesmuseum.

Schilling, Sabine (2004): *Die sozialen Themen in der Genremalerei des österreichischen Biedermeier.* Dipl.- Arb. Univ. Wien.

Weninger, Peter (1981): *Österreich. Landschaft und Mensch in Meistergemälden.* Innsbruck: Penguin-Verl. [u.a.].

3.14.2 Künstler / Artists

Fuchs, Heinrich (1972-1974): *Die Österreichischen Maler des 19. Jahrhunderts (4 Bände).* Wien: H. Fuchs [Selbstverlag].

3.14.2.1 Josef Danhauser

Birke, Veronika (Hrsg.) (1983): *Josef Danhauser: 1805- 1845. Gemälde und Zeichnungen.* (Ausst.-Kat.) Wien: Österreich. Bundesverl.

Grabner, Sabine (2011): *Der Maler Josef Danhauser. Biedermeierzeit im Bild. Monografie und Werkverzeichnis.* (Ausst.-Kat.) Wien [u.a.]: Böhlau.

Schiller, Ursula (2004): *Flämischer und holländischer Einfluß im Werk Josef Danhausers.* Dipl.- Arb. Univ. Wien.

3.14.2.2 Franz von Defregger

Ammann, Gert (1987): *Franz von Defregger und sein Kreis: Museum der Stadt Lienz auf Schloss Bruck, Städtische Galerie Lienz, im Rathaus, 13. Juni bis 20. September 1987.* (Ausst.-Kat.) Innsbruck: Tiroler Landesmuseum Ferdinandeum.

Briggs, Jo (2012): Recollection and Relocation in Gründerzeit Munich: Collective Memory and the Genre Paintings of Franz von Defregger, in: *Art history: journal of the Association of Art Historians*, Bd. 35, Nr. 1, S. 106- 126.

3.14.2.3 Eduard von Engerth

Engerth, Ruediger (1994): *Eduard Ritter von Engerth (1818- 1897). Maler, Lehrer, Galeriedirektor und Kunstschriftsteller. Beiträge zu Leben und Werk. (Forschungen und Beiträge zur Wiener Stadtgeschichte, 26).* Wien: Deuticke.

Engerth, Ruediger (1997): *Eduard von Engerth, 1818- 1897. [229. Sonderausstellung des Historischen Museums der Stadt Wien ... 18. September bis 16. November 1997].* (Ausst.-Kat.) Wien: Museen d. Stadt.

3.14.2.4 Peter Fendi

Giese, Alexander (2008): *Peter Fendi und das einfigurige Wiener Sittenbild.* Dipl.-Arb. Univ. Wien.

Koschatzky, Walter (1995): *Peter Fendi (1796- 1842): Künstler, Lehrer und Leitbild. (Graphische Sammlung Albertina <Wien>: Veröffentlichung der Albertina, Nr. 38).* Salzburg [u.a.]: Residenz-Verlag.

Schröder, Klaus Albrecht (Hrsg.) (2007): *Peter Fendi und sein Kreis*. (Ausst.-Kat.) Wien: Albertina.

3.14.2.5 Mathias Schmid

Luger, Petra R. (1999): *Mathias Schmid, 1835- 1923: ein Tiroler Maler in München*. Innsbruck: Tyrolia.

Mathias-Schmid-Museum (Hrsg.) (1999): *Mathias Schmid: (1835- 1923). Maler zwischen Paznaun und München. Ein Magazin zur Eröffnung des Mathias-Schmid-Museums in Ischgl am 2. Mai 1999 und den Mathias-Schmid-Sonderausstellungen im Tiroler Landesmuseum Ferdinandeum in Innsbruck und im Südtiroler Landesmuseum Schloß Tirol bei Meran.* Ischgl: Mathias-Schmid-Museum.

Mathias-Schmid-Museum (Hrsg.) (2002): *Mathias Schmid und die Alpen, 1835- 1923. Historienmaler, Genremaler, Zeichner und Illustrator*. Ischgl: Mathias-Schmid-Museum.

3.14.2.6 Ferdinand Georg Waldmüller

Cabuk, Cornelia (1999): Das Sittenbild als Zeitspiegel. F.G. Waldmüllers Beitrag zur Wiener Genremalerei des Biedermeier, in: *Weltkunst. Zeitschrift für Kunst und Antiquitäten*, Bd. 69, S. 912- 913.

Feuchtmüller, Rupert (1996): *Ferdinand Georg Waldmüller. 1793- 1865. Leben, Schriften, Werke*. Wien [u.a.]: Brandstätter.

Grabner, Sabine (Hrsg.) (2007): *Ferdinand Georg Waldmüller und seine Zeit*. (Ausst.-Kat.) St. Johann Herberstein: Gironcoli Museum.

Husslein-Arco, Agnes/ Grabner, Sabine (Hrsg.) (2009): *Ferdinand Georg Waldmüller: 1793- 1865*. Wien: Brandstätter.

Suppan, Martin/ Cabuk, Cornelia (1999): *Ferdinand Georg Waldmüller: Wien 1793- 1865 Mödling. Sittenmalerei im Zeitspiegel. Waldmüllers Einfluß auf die Wiener Genremalerei des Biedermeier*. Wien: Ed. Martin Suppan.

3.14.2.7 Sonstige / Others

Morath, Wolfram (Hrsg.) (1999): *Theodor Ethofer. Künstler, Kavalier, Kosmopolit. Katalog zur Sonderausstellung anlässlich seines 150. Geburtstages.* (Ausst.- Kat.) Salzburg.

Müksch, Ursula (2004): *Karl Feiertag (1874- 1944): Ein Künstlerleben. Retrospektive zum 60. Todestag. Katalog zur Ausstellung im Stadt-Museum Klosterneuburg.* (Ausst.-Kat.) Klosterneuburg: Stadtmuseum Klosterneuburg.

Oehring, Erika (Hrsg.) (2009): *Josef Engelhart: Vorstadt und Salon. (Museen <Wien>: Sonderausstellung des Wien-Museums, 356).* Wien: Brandstätter.

Strahner, Christine (2005): *Josef Wischniowsky: (1856 Pribor/Mähren – 1926 Niederndorf/Tirol). Portraitist, Orientalist, Lanschafter und Genremaler – sein Leben und Werk.* Dipl.- Arb. Univ. Innsbruck.

Strasser, Christine (1983): *August von Pettenkofen (1822- 1889). Die Szolnoker Bilder.* Diss. Univ. Salzburg.

Stutzer, Beat (Hrsg.) (2004): *Blicke ins Licht. Neue Betrachtungen zum Werk von Giovanni Segantini.* Zürich: Scheidegger & Spiess [u.a.].

3.15 Weitere europäische Länder / Other European countries

Dobrianowa-Bauer, Snegi (1999): *Auf den Spuren der Münchner Schule. Nicola Michailow und die Neue Bulgarische Malerei, 1878- 1944. (Europäische Hochschulschriften: Reihe 28, Kunstgeschichte, Bd. 332)*. Frankfurt am Main [u.a.]: Lang.

Vlček, Tomáš (1998): *Jakub Schikaneder. Maler Prags um die Jahrhundertwende. Thematischer Führer durch die retrospektive Ausstellung.* (Ausst.-Kat.) Prag.

4. Genremalerei in den USA / Genre painting in the USA

4.1 Malerei des 19. Jahrhunderts / 19th century painting

Atkinson, D. Scott/ Neff, Terry Ann R. (Hrsg.) (1987): *A proud heritage – two centuries of American art: selections from the collections of the Pennsylvania Academy of the Fine Arts, Philadelphia, and the Terra Museum of American Art, Chicago*. Chicago: Terra Museum of American Art.

Baekeland, Frederick (1991): *Images of America. The painter's eye, 1833- 1925*. (Ausst.-Kat.) Seattle [u.a.]: University of Washington Press.

Burns, Sarah/ Davis, John (2009): *American art to 1900. A documentary history*. Berkeley [u.a.]: University of California Press.

Craven, Wayne (2003): *American art. History and culture*. Boston [u.a.]: McGraw-Hill.

Davidson, Susan (Hrsg.) (2007): *Art in America. 300 years of innovation*. (Ausst.-Kat.) London [u.a.]: Merrell [u.a.].

Gaehtgens, Thomas Wolfgang (Hrsg.) (1988): *Bilder aus der Neuen Welt. Amerikanische Malerei des 18. und 19. Jahrhunderts. Meisterwerke aus der Sammlung Thyssen-Bornemisza und Museen der Vereinigten Staaten*. (Ausst.-Kat.) München: Prestel.

Gaehtgens, Thomas W./ Ickstadt, Heinz (Hrsg.) (1992): *American icons. Transatlantic perspectives on eighteenth- and nineteenth-century American art*. Santa Monica Calif. [Chicago]: Getty Center for the History of Art and the Humanities/ the University of Chicago Press.

Gallati, Barbara Dayer (Hrsg.) (2011): *Making American taste. Narrative art for a new democracy*. (Ausst.-Kat.) New York, NY: The New-York Historical Society; London: D Giles.

Groseclose, Barbara (2000): *Nineteenth century American art. (Oxford history of art)*. Oxford [u.a.]: Oxford University Press.

Koja, Stephan (Hrsg.) (1999): *America. Die Neue Welt in Bildern des 19. Jahrhunderts*. (Ausst.-Kat.) München [u.a.]: Prestel.

Lubin, David M. (1994): *Picturing a nation. Art and social change in nineteenth-century America. (Yale publications in the history of art).* New Haven [u.a.]: Yale University Press.

Luhrs, Kathleen (Hrsg.) (1994): *American paintings in the Metropolitan Museum of Art. Volume 1. A catalogue of works by artists born by 1815.* New York: Metropolitan Museum of Art in association with Princeton University Press.

Novak, Barbara (2007): *American painting of the nineteenth century. Realism, idealism, and the American experience.* 3rd ed. With a new preface. Oxford: Oxford University Press.

Tottis, James W. (Hrsg.) (2005): *Forging a modern identity: masters of American painting born after 1847.* (Ausst.-Kat.) London: Giles.

4.2 Genremalerei / Genre painting

4.2.1 Überblick / General works

Alexander Gallery, New York, N.Y. (Hrsg.) (1984): *American genre paintings: [exhibition] Alexander Gallery, New York, Feb. 14 to Mar. 14, 1984.* (Ausst.-Kat.) New York: The Gallery.

Clark, Henry Nichols Blake (1982): A taste for the Netherlands. The impact of seventeenth-century Dutch and Flemish genre painting on American art 1800-1860, in: *The American art journal*, Bd. 14, S. 23- 38.

Clark, Henry Nichols Blake (1983): *The impact of seventeenth-century Dutch and Flemish genre painting on American genre painting, 1800- 1865.* (Diss. Univ. Newark) Ann Arbor, Mich.: Univ. Microfilms Internat.

Cranbrook Academy of Art, Museum (Hrsg.) (1973): *Genre, portrait, and still life painting in America. The Victorian Era.* (Ausst.-Kat.) Bloomfield Hills, Mich.

Danly, Susan (Hrsg.) (1991): *Telling tales: Nineteenth-Century narrative painting from the collection of the Pennsylvania Academy of the Fine Arts.* New York: American Federation of Arts.

Eldredge, Charles C. (2004): *Tales from the easel: American narrative paintings from southeastern museums, circa 1800- 1950.* (Ausst.-Kat.) Athens: University of Georgia Press.

Feld, Stuart P. (1968): *The American vision. Paintings, 1825- 1875, figure and still life, genre, landscape.* (Ausst.-Kat.) New York: Galleries M. Knoedler.

Ferber, Linda S. (1982): Themes in American genre paintings: 1840- 80, in: *Apollo. The international art magazine. The international magazine for collectors*, Bd. 115, S. 250- 259.

Gallati, B.D. (2011): American genre painting and the rise of "average taste", in: *The magazine antiques*, Bd. 178, Nr. 6, S. 134- 141.

Hawes, Louis (Hrsg.) (1970): *The American scene 1820- 1900. An exhibition of landscape and outdoor genre.* (Ausst.-Kat.) Bloomington, Ind.: Art Museum.

Hills, Patricia (1974): *The painters' America. Rural and urban life, 1810- 1910.* (Ausst.-Kat.) New York: Praeger.

Hirschl & Adler Galleries (Hrsg.) (1978): *American genre painting in the Victorian era: Winslow Homer, Eastman Johnson, and their contemporaries.* (Ausst.-Kat.) New York: Hirschl & Adler Galleries.

Johns, Elizabeth (1991): *American genre painting. The politics of everyday life.* New Haven, Conn. [u.a.]: Yale University Press.

Kennedy Galleries (Hrsg.) (1977): *America past: nineteenth century landscape and genre paintings. (Kennedy quarterly, v. 15, no. 2).* New York: The Gallery.

Kennedy Galleries (Hrsg.) (1983): *American portrait, landscape, seascape, still life, and genre paintings: from 1770 to 1922 (November 1 to December 31).* New York: Kennedy Galleries.

Koke, Richard J. (Hrsg.) (1982): *American landscape and genre paintings in the New York Historical Society. A catalogue of the collection incl. historical, narrative, and marine art. (3 vol.)* New York, N.Y.: The New York Hist. Society [u.a.].

Love, Richard H./ Worley, Michael Preston (2000): *R.H. Love Galleries selections: American genre through regionalism.* Chicago: Haase-Mumm Pub. Co., distributed by Amart Book and Catalog Distributing Co.

Moure, Nancy Dustin Wall (1974): *American narrative painting.* (Ausst.-Kat.) Los Angeles: Los Angeles County Museum of Art.

Museum of Fine Arts (Saint Petersburg, Fla.) (Hrsg.) (1971): *The Good life: an exhibition of American genre painting by artists born during the first four decades of the 19th century.* (Ausst.-Kat.) St. Petersburg, Fla.: Museum of Fine Arts, St. Petersburg.

Sokol, David M. (1981): *Life in 19th century America: An exhibition of American genre painting.* (Ausst.-Kat.) Evanston, Ill.: The Museum.

Varian, Elayne H./ Luck, Robert H. (1973): *Twice as natural. 19th century American genre painting.* (Ausst.-Kat.) New York: Wittenborn Art Books.

Weinberg, H. Barabara/ Baratt, Carrie Rebora (Hrsg.) (2009): *American Stories. Paintings of Everyday Life, 1765- 1915.* (Ausst.-Kat.) New Haven, Conn. [u.a.]: Yale University Press [u.a.].

Williams, Hermann Warner (1973): *Mirror to the American past. A survey of American genre painting, 1750- 1900.* Greenwich, Conn.: New York Graphic Society.

Winer, Helen (1974): *Nineteenth century American genre painting: May- June 1974.* Albany, NY: Executive Mansion.

4.2.2 Regionale Genremalerei / Regional genre painting

Amerman, George Louis (2000): *The presence of genre painting among the works of the California impressionists.* Thesis (M.A.) Univ. California State, Dominguez Hills.

Keyes, Donald D. (1973): *Aspects of the development of genre painting in the Hudson river area before 1852.* Diss. (Ph.D.) New York University.

Sandweiss, Martha A. (1978): *Pictures from an expedition. Early views of the American West. A catalogue to accompany the exhibition from September 20, 1978, through January 6, 1979, sponsored by the Yale Center for American Art and Material Culture and the Yale University Art Gallery.* (Ausst.-Kat.) New Haven: The Gallery.

The R.W. Norton Art Gallery (Hrsg.) (1981): *Louisiana landscape and genre paintings of the 19th century: A loan exhibition, April 12- May 24, 1981, the*

R.W. Norton Art Gallery, Shreveport, Louisiana. (Ausst.-Kat.) Shreveport, La.: The Gallery.

Troccoli, Joan Carpenter (2000): *Painters and the American West. The Anschutz collection.* (Ausst.-Kat.) Denver, Colo.: Denver Art Museum.

Tyler, Ronnie C. (Hrsg.) (1987): *American frontier life: early Western painting and prints.* (Ausst.-Kat.) Forth Worth: Amon Carter Museum/ New York: Abbeville Press.

4.2.3 Spezielle Themenbereiche / Specific subject areas

Berger, Martin A. (2005): *Sight unseen. Whiteness and American visual culture.* Berkeley, Calif. [u.a.]: University of California Press.

Burns, Joseph A. (1997): *Absinthe and apathy: Late nineteenth century urban genre painting.* Thesis (M.A.) Temple Univ., Philadelphia.

Burns, Sarah (1986): Yankee Romance: The Comic Courtship Scene in Nineteenth-Century American Art, in: *American Art Journal*, Bd. 18, Nr. 4, S. 51- 75.

Connor, Holly Pyne (1996): *City-country contrasts in American genre painting, 1830- 1860.* Diss. (Ph.D.) Rutgers, the State University of New Jersey.

Da Costa Nunes, Jadviga M. (1987): The Naughty Child in Nineteenth-Century American Art, in: *Journal of American Studies*, Bd. 21, Nr. 2, S. 225- 247.

Driesbach, Janice T./ Jones, Harvey L./ Holland, Katherine Church (1998): *Art of the gold rush.* (Ausst.-Kat.) Los Angeles, Calif.: University of California Press.

Eager, Gerald (1976): The Iconography of the Boat in 19th-Century American Painting, in: *Art Journal*, Bd. 35, Nr. 3, S. 224- 230.

Edwards, Lee M. (1986): *Domestic bliss: family life in American painting, 1840- 1910.* (Ausst.-Kat.) Yonkers, N.Y.: Hudson River Museum.

Fiorino-Iannace, Giovanna P. (2004): *American genre painters in Venice. 1877- 1893.* Diss. (Ph.D.) The City University of New York.

French, Christopher C. (Hrsg.) (1990): *Facing History. The black image in American Art, 1710- 1940.* (Ausst.-Kat.) San Francisco, Calif.: Bedford Arts.

Johns, Elizabeth (1989): "This new man". National identity in mid-nineteenth-century genre painting of the United States, in: *Acts of the XXVIth International Congress of the history of art*, 3, S. 671- 678.

Kilbane, Nora C. (2006): *A tug from the jug: drinking and temperance in American genre painting, 1830- 1860*. (Diss. (Ph.D.) Ohio State University) Columbus, Ohio: Ohio State University.

O'Leary, Elizabeth L. (1996): *At beck and call. The representation of domestic servants in nineteenth-century American painting*. Washington, DC [u.a.]: Smithsonian Institution Press.

Shapiro, Emily Dana (2003): *Machine crafted: the image of the artisan in American genre painting, 1877- 1908*. Diss. (Ph.D.) Stanford University.

Tuttman, Kathe (1974): *Interior scenes of family life in American genre painting of the nineteenth century*. (Diss. Brandeis University) Waltham, Mass.

Witkowski, Terrence H. (1996): Farmers Bargaining: Buying and Selling as a Subject in American Genre Painting, 1835 to 1868, in: *Journal of macromarketing: examining the interactions among markets, marketing, and society*, Bd. 16, Nr. 2, S. 84- 101.

Wright, Lesley C. (1993): *Men making meaning in nineteenth-century American genre painting, 1860- 1900*. Diss. (Ph.D.) Stanford University.

4.3 Künstler / Artists

4.3.1 George Caleb Bingham

Adams, Henry (1983): A New Interpretation of Bingham's Fur Traders Descending the Missouri, in: *The Art Bulletin*, Bd. 65, Nr. 4, S. 675- 680.

Bloch, Maurice (1986): *The paintings of George Caleb Bingham. A catalogue raisonné*. Columbia, Mo.: University of Missouri Press.

Christ-Janer, Albert (1975): *George Caleb Bingham. Frontier painter of Missouri*. New York: Abrams.

Ehrlich, George (1978): George Caleb Bingham as ethnographer: A variant view of his genre works, in: *American Studies*, Bd. 19, Nr. 2 (A new look at old masters), S. 41- 55.

Rash, Nancy (1991): *The painting and politics of George Caleb Bingham*. New Haven [u.a.]: Yale University Press.

Saphiro, Michael Edward (1993): *George Caleb Bingham*. New York: H.N. Abrams in association with the National Museum of American Art, Smithsonian Institution.

4.3.2 John George Brown

Hoppin, Martha J. (1994): The "Little White Slaves" of New York: Paintings of Child Street Musicians by J. G. Brown, in: *American Art Journal*, Bd. 26, Nr. 1/2, S. 4- 43.

Placidi, Kathleen S. (1990): Beyond Bootblacks: "The Boat Builder" and the Art of John George Brown, in: *The Bulletin of the Cleveland Museum of Art*, Bd. 77, Nr. 10, S. 366- 382.

4.3.3 Francis William Edmonds

Clark, Henry Nichols Blake (1982): A Fresh Look at the Art of Francis W. Edmonds: Dutch Sources and American Meanings, in: *American Art Journal*, Bd. 14, Nr. 3, S. 73- 94.

Clark, Henry Nichols Blake (Hrsg.) (1988): *Francis W. Edmonds. American master in the Dutch tradition.* (Ausst.-Kat.) Washington, D.C.: Smithsonian Institution Press.

Goley, Mary Anne/ Mann, Maybelle (1976): *Francis William Edmonds: January 15 to February 15, 1976.* (Ausst.-Kat.) Washington, D.C.: Board of Governors of the Federal Reserve System.

Mann, Maybelle (1970): Francis William Edmonds: Mammon and Art, in: *American Art Journal*, Bd. 2, Nr. 2, S. 92- 106.

Mann, Maybelle (1972): *Francis William Edmonds: mammon and art*. Diss. Univ. of New York.

Mann, Maybelle (1975): *Francis William Edmonds*. (Ausst.-Kat.) Washington: International Exhibitions Foundation.

4.3.4 Seymour Joseph Guy

Lessing, Lauren (2011): Rereading Seymour Joseph Guy's *Making a Train*, in: *American Art,* Bd. 25, Nr. 1, S. 96- 111.

Weber, B. (2008): Seymour Joseph Guy: "Little Master" of American genre painting, in: *The magazine antiques*, Bd. 174, Nr. 5, S.140- 149.

4.3.5 Winslow Homer

Cikovsky, Nicolai, Jr./ Kelly, Franklin (Hrsg.) (1995): *Winslow Homer.* (Ausst.-Kat.) Washington/New Haven [u.a.]: National Gallery of Art/ Yale University Press, cop.

Giese, L. H. (2011): Winslow Homer's "Better Painting": Old Woman Gathering Faggots, 1865, in: *Visual resources: An international journal of documentation*, Bd. 27, Nr. 1, S. 63- 76.

Haltman, Kenneth (1998): Antipastoralism in Early Winslow Homer, in: *The Art Bulletin*, Bd. 80, Nr. 1, S. 93- 112.

Jennings, Kate F. (2004): *Winslow Homer*. North Dighton, Mass.: JG Press/ World Publications Group.

Johns, Elizabeth (2002): *Winslow Homer: The nature of observation*. Berkeley/ London: University of California Press.

Rash, Nancy (1995): A Note on Winslow Homer's Veteran in a New Field and Union Victory, in: *American Art,* Bd. 9, Nr. 2, S. 88- 93.

4.3.6 Thomas Hovenden

Burns, Sarah (1988): The Country Boy Goes to the City: Thomas Hovenden's "Breaking Home Ties" in American Popular Culture, in: *American Art Journal*, Bd. 20, Nr. 4, S. 59- 73.

Clark, Henry Nichols Blake (1994): *Thomas Hovenden: intimate insights.* (Ausst.-Kat.) Norfolk, Va.: Chrysler Museum.

Edwards, Lee M. (1987): Noble Domesticity: The Paintings of Thomas Hovenden, in: *American Art Journal*, Bd. 19, Nr. 1, S. 4- 38.

Terhune, Anne Gregory (1983): *Thomas Hovenden (1840- 1895) and late nineteenth-century American genre painting.* Diss. (Ph.D.) City University of New York.

Terhune, Anne Gregory (2006): *Thomas Hovenden. His life and art.* Philadelphia: University of Pennsylvania Press.

4.3.7 Henry Inman

Gerdts, William H. (1974): The Henry Inman Memorial Exhibition of 1846, in: *Archives of American Art Journal*, Bd. 14, Nr. 2, S. 2- 6.

Gerdts, William H. (1977): Henry Inman: Genre Painter, in: *American Art Journal*, Bd. 9, Nr. 1, S. 26- 48.

4.3.8 Eastman Johnson

Buick, Kirsten Pai (1990): *Eastman Johnson's "Old Kentucky Home, Negro Life at the South": from idealization to nostalgia, 1859- 1867.* Thesis (M.A.) Univ. of Michigan.

Davis, John (1998): Eastman Johnson's Negro Life at the South and Urban Slavery in Washington, D.C., in: *The Art Bulletin*, Bd. 80, Nr. 1, S. 67- 92.

Hills, Patricia Schulze (1973): *The genre painting of Eastman Johnson. The sources and development of his style and themes. In two volumes.* Diss. Univ. New York.

4.3.9 John Lewis Krimmel

Harding, Anneliese (1994): *John Lewis Krimmel. Genre artist of the early Republic.* Winterthur, Del.

Harding, Anneliese (2003): British and Scottish Models for the American Genre Paintings of John Lewis Krimmel, in: *Winterthur Portfolio*, Bd. 38, Nr. 4, S. 221- 244.

John, Richard R./ Leonard, Thomas C. (1998): The Illusion of the Ordinary: John Lewis Krimmel's Village Tavern and the Democratization of Public Life in the Early Republic, in: *Pennsylvania History*, Bd. 65, Nr. 1 (Benjamin Franklin and His Enemies), S. 87- 96.

4.3.10 William Sidney Mount

Adams, Karen M. (1975): The Black Image in the Paintings of William Sidney Mount, in: *The American Art Journal*, Bd. 7, Nr. 2, S. 42- 59.

Armstrong, Janice G. (Hrsg.) (1984): *Catching the tune. Music and William Sidney Mount.* Stony Brook, NY.

Cassedy, David/ Shrott, Gail (1983): *William Sidney Mount. Works in the collection of the museums at Stony Brook.* Stony Brook, NY.

Colbert, Charles (1994): "Fair Exchange No Robbery": William Sidney Mount's Commentary on Modern Times, in: *American Art*, Bd. 8, Nr. 3/4, S. 28- 41.

Frankenstein, Alfred Victor (Hrsg.) (1968): *Painter of rural America. William Sidney Mount, 1807- 1868.* (Ausst.-Kat.) Stony Brook, NY: Suffolk Museum.

Frankenstein, Alfred Victor (1969): William Sidney Mount and the Act of Painting, in: *American Art Journal*, Bd. 1, Nr. 1, S. 34- 42.

Frankenstein, Alfred Victor (1975): *William Sidney Mount.* New York: Abrams.

Hoover, Catherine (1981): The Influence of David Wilkie's Prints on the genre paintings of William Sidney Mount, in: *The American Art Journal*, Bd. 13, Nr. 3, S. 4- 33.

Hudson, Joseph B., Jr. (1975): Banks, Politics, Hard Cider, and Paint: The Political Origins of William Sidney Mount's "Cider Making", in: *Metropolitan Museum Journal*, Bd. 10, S. 107- 118.

Johns, Elizabeth (1986): The Farmer in the Works of William Sidney Mount, in: *The Journal of Interdisciplinary History*, Bd. 17, Nr. 1, S. 257- 281.

Johnson, Deborah J. (Hrsg.) (1998): *William Sidney Mount. Painter of American life.* New York, NY.

Katlan, Alexander (2001): William Sidney Mount's Palette and Pigments, in: *The microscope*, Bd. 49, Nr. 2, S. 111- 118.

Moffatt, Frederick C. (1994): Barnburning and Hunkerism: William Sidney Mount's "Power of Music", in: *Winterthur Portfolio*, Bd. 29, Nr. 1, S. 19- 42.

Museums at Stony Brook (Hrsg.) (1974): *An exhibition of paintings by William Sidney Mount, 1807- 1868, to commemorate the opening of the William Sidney Mount Gallery, Fine Arts Building, the Museums at Stony Brook, N.Y., October, 1974.* Stony Brook, N.Y.: The Museums.

Oedel, William T./ Gernes, Todd S. (1988): "The Painter's Triumph": William Sidney Mount and the Formation of a Middle- Class Art, in: *Winterthur Portfolio*, Bd. 23, Nr. 2/3, S. 111- 127.

Robertson, Bruce (1992): "The Power of Music": A Painting by William Sidney Mount, in: *The Bulletin of the Cleveland Museum of Art*, Bd. 79, Nr. 2, S. 38- 62.

Robertson, Bruce (1998): Who's sitting at the table?: William Sidney Mount's After Dinner 1843, in: *The Yale journal of criticism: interpretation in the humanities*, Bd. 11, Nr. 1, S. 103- 110.

Scott, Kevin Michael (2008): The Negro Touch and the Yankee Trick: William Sidney Mount and the Art of Race and Ethnicity, in: *Visual resources: An international journal of documentation*, Bd. 24, Nr. 3, S. 233- 253.

Smith, Christopher J. (2007): Ethnomusicology in oils. William Sidney Mount, "the first Atlantic street culture", and the invention of an American vernacular, in: *Music in art. International journal for music iconography*, Bd. 32, S. 189- 203.

Stanley, Marjorie Page (1997): *Politics and patronage: adumbrated ambiguity in the genre paintings of William Sidney Mount.* Thesis (B.A. with honors) Amherst College.

Suffolk Museum (Hrsg.) (1974): *Drawings and sketches by William Sidney Mount 1807- 1868 in the Collection of the Suffolk Museum & Carriage House at Stony Brook, Long Island, N.Y.* Stony Brook, NY.

4.3.11 William Ranney

Grubar, Francis S. (1970): Ranney's "The Trapper's Last Shot", in: *American Art Journal,* Bd. 2, Nr. 1, S. 92- 99.

Hassrick, Peter H. (2006): William Ranney: A Painter's Requiem to the Mountain Man, in: *Montana: The Magazine of Western History,* Bd. 56, Nr. 2, S. 42- 53.

Hassrick, Peter H. (2007): William Ranney's "Hunting Wild Horses", in: *The Southwestern Historical Quarterly,* Bd. 110, Nr. 3, S. 348- 360.

4.3.12 Lilly Martin Spencer

Bolton-Smith, Robin (1973): *Lilly Martin Spencer, 1822- 1902: The joys of sentiment.* (Ausst.-Kat.) Washington: Published for the National Collection of Fine Arts by the Smithsonian Institution Press.

Freivogel, Elsie F. (1972): Lilly Martin Spencer, in: *Archives of American Art Journal,* Bd. 12, Nr. 4, S. 9- 14.

Katz, Wendy J. (2001): Lilly Martin Spencer and the Art of Refinement, in: *American Studies,* Bd. 42, Nr. 1, S. 5- 37.

Langa, Helen (1990): Lilly Martin Spencer. Genre, aesthetics, and gender in the work of a mid-nineteenth century American woman artist, in: *Athanor,* Bd. 9, S. 37- 45.

Lubin, David M. (1993): Lilly Martin Spencer's domestic genre painting in Antebellum America, in: *American iconology. New approaches to nineteenth century art and literature,* hrsg. von David C. Miller, New Haven [u.a.]: Yale University Press, S. 135- 162.

Masten, April F. (2004): "Shake Hands?" Lilly Martin Spencer and the Politics of Art, in: *American Quarterly*, Bd. 56, Nr. 2, S. 348- 394.

Negley, Lena M. (2005): *The cult of domesticity: Examining the life and work of Lilly Martin Spencer*. Thesis (M.A.) Univ. of Wisconsin, Milwaukee.

Wierich, Jochen (2002): *War Spirit at Home*: Lilly Martin Spencer, Domestic Painting, and Artistic Hierarchy, in: *Winterthur Portfolio*, Bd. 37, Nr. 1, S. 23- 42.

4.3.13 Jerome Thompson

Edwards, Lee M. (1982): Early Jerome Thompson genre painting, in: *The American art journal*, Bd. 14, S. 72- 73.

Edwards, Lee M. (1982): The Life and Career of Jerome Thompson, in: *American Art Journal*, Bd. 14, Nr. 4, S. 4- 30.

Edwards, Lee M. (1985): Two Genre Paintings by Jerome Thompson, in: *American Art Journal*, Bd. 17, Nr. 1, S. 82- 83.

4.3.14 Richard Caton Woodville

Grubar, Francis S. (1967): *Richard Caton Woodville. An early American genre painter*. (Ausst.-Kat.) Washington, DC.

Wolff, Justin P. (1999): *Soldiers, sharps, and shills: Richard Caton Woodville and antebellum genre painting*. Diss. Princeton University.

Wolff, Justin P. (2002): *Richard Caton Woodville. American painter, artful dodger*. Princeton, NJ [u.a.]: Princeton University Press.

4.3.15 Sonstige / Others

Arkelian, Marjorie Dakin (1976): *William Hahn. Genre painter 1829- 1887*. (Ausst.-Kat.) Oakland: Museum, Art Department.

Baur, John I. H. (1969): *Three nineteenth century American painters: John Quidor – Eastman Johnson – Theodore Robinson. Catalogs of three exhibitions prepared by John I. H. Baur*. New York: Arno Press.

Carter, Denny (1978): *Henry Farny*. New York: Watson-Guptill Publications.

Chambers, Bruce W. (1980): *The world of David Gilmour Blythe (1815- 1865)*. (Ausst.-Kat.) Washington, D.C.: Published for the National Collection of Fine Arts by the Smithsonian Institution Press.

Clapper, Michael (2010): Thomas Eakins and "The Chess Players", in: *American Art*, Bd. 24, Nr. 3, S. 78- 99.

Giese, Lucretia H. (1979): James Goodwyn Clonney (1812- 1867): American Genre Painter, in: *American Art Journal*, Bd. 11, Nr. 4, S. 4- 31.

Gilbert, Barbara C. (1995): *Henry Mosler rediscovered. A nineteenth-century American- Jewish artist*. (Ausst.-Kat.) Los Angeles, Calif.

Groeschel, Harriet Hoctor (1985): *A study of the life and work of the nineteenth century artist Tompkins Harrison Matteson (1813- 1884)*. Thesis (M.A.) Syracuse University.

Hesselman, Dorothy (1998): Talking it over. A patriotic genre painting by Enoch Wood Perry, in: *Metropolitan Museum journal*, Bd. 33, S. 297- 303.

Hirschl & Adler Galleries (Hrsg.) (1978): *American genre painting in the Victorian era: Winslow Homer, Eastman Johnson, and their contemporaries*. (Ausst.-Kat.) New York: Hirschl & Adler Galleries.

Lansing, Amy Kurtz (2004): A private preserve. Edward Lamson Henry's Memories, in: *Yale University Art Gallery bulletin*, S. 97- 101.

Mathews, Nancy Mowll (1996): *Mary Cassatt: a retrospective*. Hugh Lauter Levin.

Trovaioli, August P./ Toledano, Roulhac (2008): *William Aiken Walker, southern genre painter*. Gretna: Pelican Pub. Co.

5. Asien und Südamerika / Asia and South America

5.1 Asien / Asia

Link, Howard A. (1980): *Japanese genre paintings from the Kyū sei Atami Art Museum: essays and catalogue.* Atami, Japan: The Museum.

McCausland, Shane (2010): *Telling images of China: narrative and figure paintings, 15th- 20th century from the Shanghai Museum.* London: Scala.

Morse, Anne Nishimura (Hrsg.) (2007): *Drama and desire. Japanese paintings from the floating world, 1690- 1850.* (Ausst.-Kat.) Boston, Mass.: Museum of Fine Arts.

Naumkin, Vitalij Viačeslavovič (Hrsg.) (1995): *19th century paintings of life in China.* Reading: Garnet.

5.2 Südamerika / South America

5.2.1 Mexiko / Mexico

Curiel, Gustavo/ Ramírez, Fausto/ Rubial García, Antonio (2002): *Pintura y vida cotidiana en México: siglos XVII-XX.* (Ausst.-Kat.) Seville: Fundación El Monte.

García Barragán, Elisa (1998): *José Agustín Arrieta: Lumbres de lo cotidiano.* Coyoacán, México, D.F.: Fondo Editorial de la Plástica Mexicana.

Lara, Linda (2007): *José Agustín Arrieta: Beyond the quotidian in nineteenth-century Mexican costumbrista painting.* Thesis (M.A.) Univ. of California, Los Angeles.

Moyseén, Xavier (1965): *Pintura popular y costumbrista del siglo XIX.* Mexico: Artes de Mexico.

Pinacoteca Marqués del Jaral de Berrio/ Fomento Cultural Banamex (Hrsg.) (1977): *People and landscapes of nineteenth century Mexico: [exhibition] Marqués del Jaral de Berrio Pinakothek, Fomento Cultural Banamex, November-December, 1977.* Mexico City: Fomento Cultural Banamex.

www.ingramcontent.com/pod-product-compliance
Lightning Source LLC
Chambersburg PA
CBHW070314230526
45470CB00002B/874